Audacious Poetry
Reflections of Adolescence

70 Poems • Activities • Insights

by
Greta Barclay Lipson, Ed.D.

with consultant
Mark B. Lipson, M.S.W.
School Social Worker

illustrated by Susan Kropa

Cover by Christopher C. Rundell

Copyright © 1992, Good Apple

ISBN No. 0-86653-683-3

Printing No. 987654321

Good Apple
1204 Buchanan St., Box 299
Carthage, IL 62321-0299

SIMON & SCHUSTER *A Paramount Communications Company*

Dedication

This book is for my younger brother, Mel, of the elegant mind–
Who delivers babies lovingly and with hope for their future
Who works toward an enlightened and humane world
Whose interests and talents are astonishing in all their variety
Who, in his precious spare time, reads poetry
and whom I love and admire with all my heart.

Blessings on his head.

GA1417

Table of Contents

GA1417

Poems That Speak for Themselves

For the Teacher

This is a book for and about adolescents. It contains seventy funny and honest poems that trace the concerns of adolescents, their problems, dilemmas and celebrations in a fresh and lighthearted style. The material acts as a guided trip through moods, friends, teen-speak, parents, fashion, self-doubt and a multiplicity of issues which beset this transformational time of life.

Each poem speaks to the essential stuff of students' daily lives, in and out of school. The insightful themes of the transitional years are linked to activities which bind the adolescent experience into finely tuned lessons for writing and discussion in the classroom.

At the end of the book there are "Poems That Speak for Themselves" that do not include activities. You are invited to use these in whatever ways suit you and your students. Like all the other poems they express the adolescent experience and invite reflection, laughter, consternation and a recognition of the human drama.

They Are Your Children and Mine

by Dr. Paul D. Paparella

They have the battle of Lexington on their laps, cradling matchstick forts and tin soldiers who march and drum to the rhythm of the bus, lacrosse sticks held high, hockey sticks searching for the elusive puck, bowling balls wrapped like giant eggs in cotton, water pistols leaking in their pockets, firecrackers spilling powder into jacket linings, poison pen letters yellowing in their jeans, gum wrappers metamorphosed in bracelets, magic markers the color of graffiti, and an occasional book to betray their destination.

Who are they? They are your children. And mine. They look like us. They share our names. They carry our hopes and their dreams on shoulders more than a boy's, less than a man's, more than a girl's, less than a woman's.

They can bully and brag and be cruel. They can cry over a rumor, laugh uncontrollably over nothing, smile to cover their hurt, and amaze us at how quickly they can move from one emotion to another.

They run instead of walk, shout instead of whisper, forget their lunch, their money, their homework, all too often. The lost and found table groans under the weight of boots, sneakers, pocketbooks, retainers in plastic cups, sweaters, gym shorts, baseball gloves, jackets, notebooks, textbooks, but not one single example of that relic from our day—the earmuff. (And they say times haven't changed.)

They carry enough collective wire in their mouths to tilt the world several more degrees off its axis. They can find a contact lens within a radius of a thousand feet and not be able to avoid that one wet spot in an empty hallway. They can sit absolutely silent in a crowded gymnasium when one of their peers attempts a dangerous stunt on the uneven bars. They can cook and sew, publish a newspaper, put together a yearbook, handle tools dangerous enough for a grown-up, make the honor roll, come to school with a cold, catch the measles, lose their first fight, have their first boyfriend or girlfriend, flunk their first test, dissect their first anything, grow inches, gain pounds, and leave in two years in a different body from the one in which they entered. They spend their junior high years shedding the impostors who changed every second, every minute, every hour, every day, every month, searching constantly for their real selves.

GA1417

They do get tired and hurt, and they need a kind word or look from us more often than you think. They will walk for charity, bike in any bike-a-thon, drink more water than a camel, disco themselves into shin splints, and then come to physical education with a medical excuse. They will eat a potato chip and Dorito® lunch, topped off by Italian ice and a Twinkie® and six containers of chocolate milk. They store enough sandwiches in their lockers to feed a continent, and they have proved without a doubt that peanut butter does turn into stone when tucked away in a locker for six months.

They play for our athletic teams in rain and snow, wallow in mud, and break bones–all in front of a very few people. They can play music with a talent beyond their years. They fit everything in among orthodontist appointments, religion classes, piano lessons, ballet lessons, gymnastic lessons, ice skating lessons, measles, mumps, chicken pox, family quarrels, family celebrations, and homework. They are not made of steel. They have serious illnesses, spend time in the hospital, and suffer from perhaps the most serious ailment for all adolescents, a broken heart. They experience family discord, family illness, and death in the family. They find comfort in a friend, support from peers, and we hope, love and understanding from us.

Who are they? They are your children. And mine. They look like us. They share our names. And they spend most of their lives away from our direct influence. But our indirect influence in the form of directions planted and love given will remain with them to comfort and guide them for the rest of their days. The greatest sign of a successful teacher or parent is not what the student or child did while in the classroom, or in the home, but what he or she does with his or her life when we are a memory or a phone call away. May that memory never be too faint or that phone too busy.

Paul Paparella (1979). "They Are Your Children and Mine," *Educational Leadership*, 37, 2: 169-170. Reprinted with permission of the Association for Supervision and Curriculum Development. Copyright © 1979 by ASCD. All rights reserved.

Glands Run Amok

Psychology books are now quite alarming
They describe adolescents as not very charming

They tell us that glands, which we cannot see,
Can cause lots of weirds and much misery

Adolescence is a product of the industrial revolution*
It was the second disaster right after pollution

When adolescence was first invented
Folks tried their best but couldn't prevent it.

It is just nature's way—and biological luck
That this is the time that glands run amok!

It strikes the pubescent population
And puts parents and teachers in a tough situation

Sometimes these teens act like ordinary people
And other times like there's bats in their steeple

This is due to a physiological clock
Which makes some kids go tick, and others go tock.

So—while dudes and dudettes join together in cult-hood
You can always look forward to their upcoming adulthood

Hooray, for informed endo-crin-ologists
Who predict the course of pubescent chronologists
And provide information but not as apologists
When glands run amok in our land!

Greta B. Lipson

---

*Roy J. Hopkins. *Adolescence: The Transitional Years*, Academic Press, A subsidiary of Harcourt Brace Jovanovich. New York, 1983, p. 313.
*G. Lipson and E. Lipson, *Everyday Law for Young Citizens*, Good Apple, Inc., Carthage, Illinois, 1988, p. 41.

Activities

- When considering "unconditional love," it is very comfortable to think about the love of dogs for their owners. *Unconditional* means "without conditions or reservations." It means absolute love. It is certain that pets offer love without regard to race, color, creed, or good looks! And this kind of love can be most reassuring. Does unconditional love have any drawbacks? Explain.

- To what degree should families offer this kind of love? Should there be limits in families no matter what the circumstances might be? What is the difference between the unconditional love of pets, family members, and friends?

- What kinds of loyalties do you expect from your friends? How much are you prepared to give as a friend? What would make you withdraw your support? Explain. Respond to each question separately.

- Find pictures of pets and people and match them up according to your notion of who belongs to whom. An unforgettable classic match is that of the World War II Prime Minister Winston Churchill and an English bulldog. (The bulldog is the one without a cigar in his mouth!)

- In the introduction to his book *The Company of Dogs* the author, Michael J. Rosen, theorizes that, because dogs love humans so much, canines have lost their integrity. "They've been true to us, yes, but they haven't been true to themselves." How could this statement transfer over to a human relationship as it regards total and complete love for another person?

Doggone Right

If a dog loves you:

You've never known
Such love before
She's blind to your faults
Though you may be a bore.

What's more—
She doesn't care if
You're not a grand prince
Or a raggedy pauper
Or incredibly rich.

She believes in equality
Ignores color or creed
She didn't pick you
Because of your breed.

As for brains she won't care
That you're hopelessly dense
With the style of a boor
And the sense of a fence!

She doesn't care if you're handsome
Or pretty—
Naive from the country
Or slick from the city

So respect that affection
That endures like no other
'Cause she probably loves you
Much more than your brother!

Greta B. Lipson

2A

GA1417

Activities

• Research the current guidelines for nutrition with regard to fat, saturated fat, sugar, sodium, cholesterol content in food, and acceptable quantities of protein intake. Produce a usable "Nutrition Fact Sheet" based upon the information you gathered. Some adolescents can eat tremendous amounts of food and not gain weight, the reason being that their metabolisms are very high and can easily burn their high caloric intake. Other adolescents may develop weight problems which are very difficult to cope with, as most Americans know. But both of these groups, fat and thin, may be uninformed about proper nutrition which sets the stage for a lifetime of bad eating habits and related health problems.

• Imagine that you encounter a civilization called "Doofus" where everything that is considered bad food in our culture is considered to be nutritious in theirs. Develop a menu for the day or week in that wonderfully weird culture. Breakfast may consist of a cream puff, hot fudge sundae, 10 ounces of soda pop, and a bag of potato chips with dip. Have a good time while you can and go the whole hog!

• American diets tend to be extremely high in fats and sugars while being very low in essential vitamins and nutrients. Rates of heart disease and cancer in this country are much higher than in countries where the consumption of fats, especially animal fats, is much lower. With the help of your librarian, research the differences in diet in America as contrasted to Italy and Japan. Chart the resulting differences in the health profile as it relates to heart disease, cancer, diabetes, and hypertension. What other startling differences did you find along the way that relate to diet and its effect over a lifetime? Why are adolescents often indifferent to the long-term effects of bad eating habits? (To the Teacher: The students believe they are invincible and will live forever–right?)

• Find a calorie chart that is age appropriate for you and learn to use it!

Beware the Food Police

The food police are coming if you don't watch out
They're looking for the likes of you–they want to hunt you out.

There are penalties for folks like you who never give a fig
For what you eat, they'll lock you up with other little pigs.

Yellow cakes and pretzels and candy crunch that's tough
Marshmallows and toffee and caramel corn that's rough

With butter fat and frosting and sugar you adore
You'll narrow down your arteries and clog up all your pores.

Hot dogs will link a crimson rope that snakes all through your gizzard
The hamburgers will pile in stacks and grease up all your innards.

Potato chips will float around and deaden up your brain
While melted nougat starts to ooze into your body's drain.

Your waistline will get bigger–your fat will flop and wiggle
Your belt will cut off all your breath; your cells will bulge and jiggle.

It's bad for you, it's bad for you–this sugar, salt and fat!
Give up hot fudge and evil ways and be a healthy chap!

Reform, repent, redeem yourself–the food police are rough
But they will not be quite so tough if you give up this rotten stuff!

Greta B. Lipson

GA1417

Activities

- Do you agree or disagree that the person in this poem, who is madly in love, would have the insight to realize that "this attraction isn't right" or "you're not too bright" or "your idle chatter is a bore"? When people are very much in love, are they able to see the love object in a rational way?

- How would you define *love at first sight*? What are the chances that this kind of attraction can survive the test of time between two people? Explain. You may want to look at a modern language version of Shakespeare's young lovers in *Romeo & Juliet: Plainspoken* (published by Good Apple, Inc.). Why is the four-day love affair between Romeo Montague, a sixteen-year-old, and Juliet Capulet, a thirteen-year-old, convincing? Write your own critical review of such a happening.

- On occasion we try to save a friend from a bad relationship. List the kinds of things that can happen when you interfere in a friend's romantic or platonic attachment to someone?

- What is the difference between a crush, infatuation, and real love? Look at a dictionary entry and then define these conditions.

- Why does parental interference in affairs of the heart cause trouble? When have you disagreed vigorously with your parents even though you knew they were right? Why, then, did you disagree? How did other feelings toward your parents cloud the issue? Write a paragraph describing such a conflict over the choice of friends. Role-play an imaginary argument of this kind.

4

Is This Love or Stupidity?

How do I love thee?
How am I supposed to know?
I've never felt so miserable before.

I love your hair, your teeth, your nose,
I even love your baggy clothes
It's Cupid and not me who knows the score.

This attraction isn't right,
'Cause it's clear you're not too bright
And what's worse your idle chatter
Is a bore!

When I get back my senses
I will build up my defenses
And I'll boot that crazy Cupid
Through the door.

Until then, oh dearest darling,
Precious one, sublimest starling
You're the only one this second
I adore!

Greta B. Lipson

GA1417

Activities

- Does the act of crying in public have anything to do with being a male or a female? If you believe it does or does not have something to do with gender, explain your position.

- If it is perfectly acceptable to laugh when you're happy, why is it less acceptable to cry when you are overcome with sadness? List the (private) reasons why a person may sometimes try very hard not to show grief or pain publicly by crying.

- When you give expression to sadness, when you bring such feelings to the surface, when you give yourself permission to let go of your conscious grief, does it make you feel better or worse? Why?

- Describe a situation at the movies similar to the one in the poem. What movie did you see, and what triggered the personal waterfall?

- Write about an incredibly happy experience that made you cry. Use the heading "Boohoo with Joy." Did it happen at a sports event, a contest, an airline terminal, in church, in the hospital, at a meeting? In the same category, have you ever been laughing hard only to discover that your laughter has turned to crying? How would you explain such a strange turn of events?

- Make up a serious or humorous song title or lyrics involving crying. One from the old days went something like this: "I have tears in my ears, lying on my back, crying over you."

GA1417

Blubbering at the Movies

The movie was a killer
And it put me to the test
With pain and grief
Just pouring off the screen

Two hours without relief
And the ending wasn't brief
'Cause everybody died except the dog.

The hound whose name was Rover
Was later crossing over
On a treacherous configurated road
When a missile from the sky
Struck his head
He said good-bye–
And I struggled with a sense of disbelief!

Oh I blubbered and I cried
As he lay upon his side
And the violins were playing rich and strong

Crimson nose and swollen face
Teary eyes I couldn't erase
How I prayed I would be hidden in the dark.

Then at once the lights revealed
What I wanted to conceal:
I was moved by the sad story on the screen.

Silence filled the air
I discovered that I shared
(with red noses that were there)
The compassionate capacity to care!

Greta B. Lipson

GA1417

Activities

- A school dance can be unpleasant and not much fun for some people. Form drama groups, and role-play a situation in front of the class. Plan a dance that would really be fun for everybody, not just the few popular characters at school. Arrange for some details that would make the event a happy experience for everybody. Will it be a dance to raise funds for something, a contest for ugly dogs, a "come as you are" party, or what? Of course, you can be serious but certainly be imaginative!

- How would you make a person more at ease who was feeling awkward at a school dance? List some of the strategies you could use to make the situation more comfortable for your friend?

- There are two different perspectives in this poem. Write a statement about the adult voice in this piece (who does not seem to understand that students can have social problems and difficulties at dances). What are some of the things you would try to explain?

- The word *angst* in the poem means "anxiety." If you were to make a list of some of the concerns young people have about teenage social functions, how many items could you include? What are these concerns? Are there some you think are foolish?

- What would account for the many different attitudes toward school dances? Would some people be right and other people wrong, or would it simply be a matter of different perceptions from one person to the next? Conduct a panel discussion analyzing these conflicting attitudes.

- If you have the courage to laugh at yourself, write a "journal entry" of something really funny, embarrassing, or goofy that happened to you at a school dance. Or perhaps, as an innocent observer, you had a good laugh because of something you saw.

Fun at the Dance

(Old Voice)

Oh have a good time at the dance
My dear,
For the young are the light of heart
Oh have a good time at the dance
My dear,
From here sweet memories start.

(Young Voice)

Oh what about angst at the dance, my dear
I'm afraid of so many things
My mind is so full of such dread, my dear
For the pain that the dance will bring.

(Young Voice)

For the young are not truly so light of heart
It's a lie the older ones sing
It is here that illusions fall apart
With the dreams that the young ones bring.

(Old Voice)

You create your bad time at the dance, I fear
For you are not light of heart
You will have a sad time at the dance, my dear
With your gnawing self-doubt from the start.

Greta B. Lipson

GA1417

Activities

• Are you the oldest child, the middle child, the youngest, or the only child? There are different conditions that go along with your "birth order." From your point of view, list some of the advantages and disadvantages of each place in the family. Does the oldest have more responsibility? Does everyone pick on the middle child? Is the baby always indulged?

• What if you had to advertise in the classified section of your newspaper for a baby-sitter for your baby brother or a tutor for the oldest kid in the family? How would you word the advertisement to make them sound fun to be with or just good kids? Obviously you have had to rethink your attitudes and consider their good points in your descriptions of them.

• Perhaps you are feeling particularly mean and want to place an ad to sell one of your siblings. How would that ad read?

• If you were to fill out a complaint form, how would it look? Look at the example and then design a form that you believe tells the whole story.

I do not receive enough

_____ love

_____ attention

_____ credit

_____ cooperation

_____ understanding

_____ privacy

Who gets more of the above? Why? What would you suggest as a solution?

GA1417

Siblings on Parade

I have a brother
Whose mouth is so wide
He can talk, chew, and slurp
With a pizza inside.

I have a sister
With makeup so bright
She gets ready for school
And looks like a fright.

There's a baby at home
Who is dumb as a door
He's dirty and grungy
And slops up the floor.

My parents are lucky
There are few, it would seem
As perfect as I
Except in a dream.

Perfection is mine
Yet I'm humble as pie
What's that you say?

"It's a horrible lie!"

Greta B. Lipson

7A

Activities

- Once again we learn about the relative standards of beauty. What is attractive to one person may be most unattractive to another. We are born into a culture in which the definition of *beauty* is well established. Pretend that you are an alien from outer space. Describe yourself in detail: facial features (if you have a face), body characteristics, and other comprehensive details. Based on that description, what do you consider to be ugly when you visit planet Earth and see humans for the first time? In front of the class try your best to describe these disgusting looking earthlings to your friend, whose name is Gip. Your home planet is Krop, somewhere on the outer limits!

- Many years ago on the TV series *Twilight Zone* there appeared a brief skit which would be an excellent role-play drama for students to demonstrate the theme that beauty is culturally defined. Reconstructed for classroom use: Several doctors and nurses are with a patient who has had plastic surgery. The medical team's faces are not visible. (Their backs are to the class.) They slowly unwind the bandages from the patient and are thrilled with the beautiful and successful result. When the patient is exposed to the class, he is undeniably ugly (your choice of strange characteristics). When the medical team turns to face the class, they too are weird looking. The logistics of this improvisational drama can be challenging and startling!

- What do you consider to be a good date or an interesting time with a friend? Make a list (short or long) of the factors that matter for your comfort and enjoyment. What things are a definite turnoff?

- Write a paragraph entitled "First Impressions." Are you inclined to make snap judgements about people? Do you give them a second chance? How dependable are these quick reactions? How do you think you impress people at a first meeting? Can you recall a time when you acted like a nitwit and wondered whatever made you do it? What do you think was the reason for your behavior?

GA1417

Blind Date

HE:
I walked up to the door
With anxiety galore
Just hoping this would be
    a perfect date.

The door swung into space
When I looked into her face
Confirming the old treachery
    of fate.

I saw her from the side
And I tried my best to hide–
Too late to run away
    or hesitate.

    SHE:
    I walked up to the door
    With anxiety galore
    Just hoping this would be
        a human date.

    The door swung into space
    And revealed his greenish face
    A wrinkled frog all warts
        from top to toe.

HE:
I am Royalty, you see
So it's really up to me
To pick and choose a bride
    who complements!

You are pretty, but I fear
That your skin is far too clear,
For amphibians
    out looking for a mate!

        Greta B. Lipson

GA1417

Activities

- Since many students do not dress conservatively, do you believe that proves that young people are nonconformists in matters of fashion? How could it be argued to the contrary that students are very serious conformists in matters of fashion? List reasons to support both points of view.

- The fashion poem is written in a military marching cadence. For what reason would the writer choose this particular style for a poem whose subject is fashion? (The implication of the herd intellect, all marching in step, is a metaphor for the way adolescents observe and follow fads and fashions, always moving with the crowd.)

- We cannot forget our debt to the Bavarian immigrant Levi Strauss (1829-1902). He traveled to San Francisco during the Gold Rush with bolts of canvas intended for equipment for Conestoga wagons. Instead, he made trousers out of the material–responding to the need of the rough and tough gold prospectors. The rest is history. What piece of clothing could you invent that would generate popular demand? The garment would have your name attached–just like the eponyms Levi's and leotards. Try it!

- A *fad* is defined as "a fashion that seems to spring up out of nowhere." It catches on fast; a lot of people are attracted to it and will go along with it. Almost as fast as it appears, its attractiveness is exhausted and the style disappears. What is the ugliest fad in fashion that you can remember? What is the ugliest fad that the adults in your family can remember? Make up a fad for males, females, or unisex. If the class is courageous enough, organize a fashion show in which the judges award a prize for "The Best in Ugliness."

- "Sloppy dressers have sloppy minds!" Is that true? Write two letters to the editor of an imagined daily paper expressing both pro and con attitudes.

Fashion March

LEFT RIGHT–LEFT RIGHT
what are we going to wear tonight?
tall short–thin stout
what's this madness all about?

LEFT RIGHT–LEFT RIGHT
the chains I feel
are far too tight
the rules are tough
don't try to fight!

LEFT RIGHT–LEFT RIGHT
conform to styles
with all your might!
sometimes we look
like quite a fright!

LEFT RIGHT–LEFT RIGHT
style changes
over night!
whoever's boss
is full of spite!

LEFT RIGHT–LEFT RIGHT
we're always in
a desperate plight!
but still we can't
give up the fight

LEFT RIGHT–LEFT RIGHT

Greta B. Lipson

GA1417

Activities

- Having friends validates a person's sense of identity and self-worth. Discuss and then rank in order the important attitudes in a friendship. For example:

    Sharing happy and bad times

    Being a giving person and not a taker

    Being kind and tactful in criticism when appropriate

    Being accepting of the differences in personality

    Respecting confidences

    Allowing your friend to have other friends without being possessive

    Having enough integrity to argue but knowing when to stop

    Respecting opinions that are different from yours

    Being forgiving and understanding

- If the isolated and despairing student in the poem came to you for advice on how to make friends, what would your answer be?

- Develop a "concept lyric" about friendship. In small groups, students will discuss their definitions of a friend. Each contribution will be added to a working paper entitled "What Is a Friend?" Everyone in the group may contribute a phrase which describes a friend. List as many poetic (nonrhyming) phrases as are suggested. Select the ten best phrases and put them in the most effective order. End the lyric with "That is a friend!"

Example:

    What is a friend?

    > As solid as a rock
    > Always there in all kinds of weather
    > Two good ears and a heart for listening

    That is a friend!*

- To develop a warm sense of community, conduct an "Applause, Applause" session. Invite volunteers to stand in front of the class and tell something they recently did for themselves or another person that was really nice (cleaned your room without being nagged). The teacher may lead off the event. When the person finishes, everyone in class stands and applauds vigorously. That person chooses another person to stand and be applauded in a brief, well-timed activity.

---

*From Greta B. Lipson, *Fast Ideas for Busy Teachers* (Carthage, Illinois: Good Apple, Inc. 1989), p. 37.

Friendless

Can you keep a desperate secret?
I am needy and yearning for a friend.

I am a solitary figure
As I walk along–pretending
That I am on my way
To meet with friends

They pass me by in groups and clusters
Moving in and out of classrooms
Purposeful and animated
Perfectly attuned

No one as lonely as I, in this crowd
All the while the rise and fall of conversation
And laughter–which clangs
In the empty chambers of my heart

Looking down the cavernous corridors
I imagine the hallways lined with fun-house mirrors
In which everyone is reflected with friends
      in duplicated harmonies

Only I am reflected alone
In an infinity of loneliness.
Where is there someone for me?

Or is there no one?

Greta B. Lipson

GA1417

Activities

- The poem speaks about change and suggests that there is much over which we have no control. What do you think will be some of the most dramatic changes in your life? (Don't forget the changes from childhood to adolescence to adulthood!)

- How can change be exciting to some people and upsetting to others? Do you always associate change with good things, bad things, or both? Is it possible that an unhappy change can turn into something really good?

- In a paragraph describe a change you have seen which you consider to be the most dramatic. It may be in your own small world—among your friends, at school, in your environment—in fashion, politics or in the world at large.

- Thomas Wolfe, a famous American author (1900-1938), wrote a book entitled *You Can't Go Home Again*. That title has become a byword. What do you think the title means? Use the chalkboard to record the interpretations of the class. (Once having left your childhood home, you can never return as the person you once were and recapture the warmth, the associations, the sights, and sounds. For not only has "home" changed, but you have changed as well. Everything and everybody changes.)

- Think of the best friend you have. Imagine that person having to move away. If you were to write a sincere letter expressing your sense of loss or grief, what would you write in that letter? How would the lack of control over life's events affect your feelings in this situation?

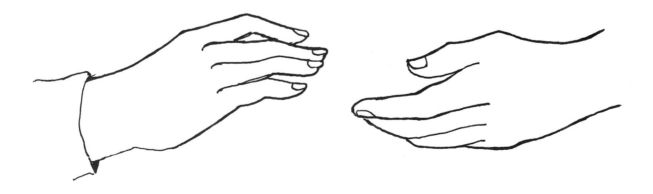

11

GA1417

Good-Bye, Old Buddy

There would be nothing in the world to separate us!

We promised that to one another.
A constancy that none could wrench apart.
This was no casual pact we made
Not children's play!

We promised from the heart
That we would grow into maturity together
With all the changes that would come
Which we would weather
As partners we could learn about the world.

Our parents could not know
(Nor would they try to remember)
A bond as strong as ours
Which they, perhaps, did share in early years long passed.

But they did not deride our loyalty
For we lived side-by-side
Since we were small

And then the tragic blow did smite!

The sign went up to signal our distress,
Pounded into the ground–
As painful as a shaft
Driven into the chest.

It said, "This House for Sale."

Greta B. Lipson

GA1417

Activities

- Despite what advertisements tell us, perfection is not attainable! But if you could be like someone else, who would that person be and what are the reasons for your choice? What does it mean to have a positive role model?

- Relative to the topic of wanting to be somebody else, what would you say is the greater meaning suggested by the following poem about Richard Cory?

RICHARD CORY*
Whenever Richard Cory went down town,
We people on the pavement looked at him:
He was a gentleman from sole to crown,
Clean favored, and imperially slim.

And he was always quietly arrayed,
And he was always human when he talked;
But still he fluttered pulses when he said,
"Good morning," and he glittered when he walked.

And he was rich—yes, richer than a king—
And admirably schooled in every grace;
In fine, we thought that he was everything
To make us wish that we were in his place.

So on we worked, and waited for the light,
And went without the meat, and cursed the bread;
And Richard Cory, one calm summer night,
Went home and put a bullet through his head.
                          Edwin Arlington Robinson
                                (1869-1935)

- We are told that physically beautiful people have their own set of problems and are not always happy. Imagine some of the difficulties people could have who seem to "have it all." Though you may not be very sympathetic toward beautiful people, imagine how the attitude of others could make their lives miserable. Try to account for these attitudes and then discuss them. What are your conclusions?

---

*Reprinted courtesy of Charles Scribner's Sons, from *Children of the Night*.

 GA1417

If I Could Be like Somebody Else

If my hair were somewhat longer
And my curls were loose and blonder

If my eyes were big and bluer
And my teeth were white and truer

If my dimples weren't inverted
And my ears weren't so perverted
     Would my life be more successful right away?

Were I soulful and more serious
Would that make me more mysterious?

If my grip were so much tighter
And I acted like a fighter

If my skills were much more sporting
And my muscles more cavorting
     Would my life be more successful right away?

Were I big and not so small
Lank and lean, long and tall

If my brains were super large
And it gave the class a charge

Were I funny and so witty
And the toast of the whole city
     Would my life be more successful right away?

The truth is: I am I!
And the best thing I can do
Is be comfortable and free–
With the one who's really me.

Greta B. Lipson

GA1417

Activities

- It's show time! A group of students are going to put together a funny skit based upon the sage advice of Dr. Shrink, a child psychologist who writes for the *Daily Blabber*. The good doctor has given tips on what to take to keep the children happy and amused in the back seat on your upcoming motor trip. Arrange chairs to mock up the interior of your car, complete with the appropriate toys, games, and other instruments of parental torture. Your parent is at the wheel. You may start with a brief lecture given by Dr. Shrink, assuring that her suggestions will help maintain sanity while traveling!

- It is easy to go along on a trip planned by someone else and complain and gripe all the way. So–you do the planning this time for a fabulous, fantasy trip. You must provide information from beginning to end. Where will you go? How will you get there (car, boat, plane)? What travel agent, if any, will you consult? What would the fare, gasoline, or other travel arrangements cost? Describe land arrangements, geographic location, and temperature. What is the cost of your living accommodations once you arrive? What activities are available to you on your dream vacation? Do you want to take a chance and guarantee everyone a good time?

- Do you agree or disagree with the following statements? Explain your answers. What complaint would you add to the following list?

  ☐ Being with the family interferes with your new sense of independence.
  ☐ Having to go suggests that you still have the status of a young child.
  ☐ You never have a voice or a choice in the planning.
  ☐ Home alone is a more interesting place to be.
  ☐ Traveling by car is boring and that's why you fight with your siblings.
  ☐ You don't want to miss out on the fun things your friends are doing.

- Role-play a family scene in which the entire family is present and the planning is a democratic process. Everyone is free to offer a suggestion, or an alternative plan. The only provision is that the suggestions must be sensible, manageable, and within the family budget. Following the role play, did you have the impression that every family member was pleased with the result? Why would (or wouldn't) this democratic approach work in your house?

13

GA1417

Family Vacation

It's vacation time in our lives TRA LA
When the birds and the scenery's sweet
The family's stuffed in the car again
For our usual summertime treat.

It's holiday time in our lives TRA LA
When the deer and the antelope roam
We'll be fighting the discord, frustration and heat
How I wish they had left me at home.

It's touring time in July TRA LA
But from me they can never disguise
The wear and the tear of our wartime fatigue
Which we kids do profoundly despise!

It's togetherness time for the bunch TRA LA
A summer of earthly delights
The worst of our rotten tempers flare
And that's when we have our best fights.

Greta B. Lipson

13A

GA1417

Activities

- Read the following to the class:

This poem is about territoriality and the importance of having one's own space which is an extension of the self. The protection of one's territory, however limited, gives the assurance of a retreat or a sacred domain, closed and safe from interlopers. There are also obvious "control" issues at stake here. The room is symbolic of the self, while the parents' demands to keep it clean are viewed as another example of parents trying to exert control over the adolescent. Though the room may belong to the adolescent, the home belongs to the parent, and while ownership may be fairly contested by all parties, the right to privacy is a critical necessity for young and old alike. There are other rights involved as well, such as freedom of expression and the right to keep one's room in whatever style or condition one pleases.

- It is possible to have strong feelings about a situation on an intuitive level and to feel you are right, without having sorted through the issues that are involved. The preceding paragraph highlights some of these issues. In listening to the paragraph, what did it clarify and what do you think should be included in matters relative to your own room (personal space, parental conflict, territoriality, sacred retreat, privacy, freedom of expression)?

- In a written description (illustrations optional) tell what your dream room would be like if you had the resources. Include any technology that would enhance your privacy, such as a closed circuit TV to inform you of approaching visitors.

- For a harrowing story using the theme of a kid's room, locate "The Veldt" by the great science fiction writer Ray Bradbury. Have it presented to the class by a reader who can deliver the story with drama and chills.

- The psychological term *proxemics* refers to personal territoriality. Split the class into two groups facing each other from a distance. One line stands still while the other line walks toward the first. As soon as the stationary person feels uncomfortable with the close proximity of the person coming forward, say "stop." This comfortable distance is culturally defined. What else does it tell you?

Whose Dirty Room Is This Anyway?

Wait just a minute!

I don't interfere with your place in this house–
       so don't interfere with mine.
I need privacy of my own too.
My room is my room.

It's my hideaway, my den, my lair, my cave
       my desert isle, my retreat, my swamp
And I'm the creature from the dank pit.

The sludge makes me feel welcome
The junk, the bags, old flags, posters, banners, signs,
       old socks and rocks.
Nobody's standards for livability but mine!

Some day, if I do not appear and you are afraid for my survival,
Open the door gently and throw in a safety line–
       with a half hitch knot–for my waist.

And it will wind its way through the rubbish with a
       serpentine intuition for finding lost, adventurous souls,
Past detritus and mechanical innards and arrive at the place of
       the multicolored "jaw breakers" in the gum ball machine
       I bought from Mr. Polokoff.

When he asked, "So where will you put it?"
       and I said, "In my room."

          he said, "Such a good idea!"

So please–remember–
My room is my room.

Greta B. Lipson

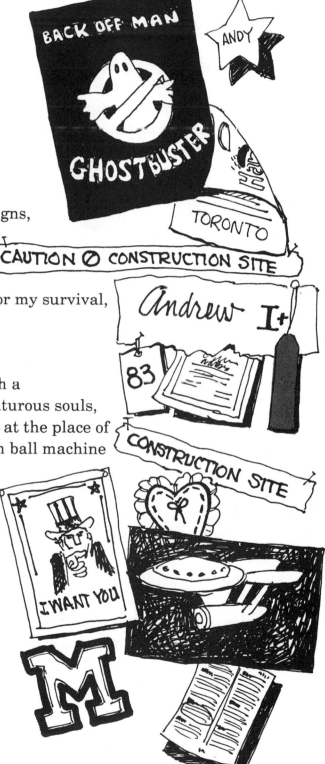

Activities

- Some behaviors seem to be residual behaviors from the animal kingdom which establishes a pecking order among its members by physical size, aggression, dominance, and other characteristics. In humans and other species, these traits give their owners more status, power, territory and other rights within their community. It should be noted that the greatest strength, creativity, and wisdom are most fully achieved by the willingness to find solutions for the greater good rather than for self-aggrandizement. Write a one-page account of the most intense conflict you have experienced. Conclude the paper with a suggestion for resolving the problem without a fight. There are research programs and methods for students regarding "conflict resolution" and student mediation, done by students without adult intervention.* For more information write: National Center for Dispute Settlement, 5530 Wisconsin Ave., #1130, Chevy Chase, MD 20815, 301-654-6515.

- Role-play four conflict situations which occur most frequently in school. After the presentation, open up the discussion to the class, asking the questions: How could the behavior of the antagonists have been modified to avoid the hostile confrontation? What are your suggestions for a peaceful settlement of the situation?

- On a piece of paper, select one or more people in your class whom you trust to do a good job of resolving conflicts. What recommends those you have chosen for the job? Assume that peer counseling was available in your school. Discuss the personality traits needed by student counselors to mediate problems effectively? List the qualifying criteria on the chalkboard and rank order them in terms of what is absolutely required for the task.

- Though we do our best to avoid fights in daily living, it is interesting to read about the ethics of professional boxing in the ring. Recently a professional fight was stopped "early" by a referee—to the outraged disappointment of the paying patrons who felt cheated! A boxing analyst, Larry Merchant, wrote an article in the *New York Times* in which he stated his two criteria on which to judge when a fight is over: "1) A fighter is being punished, and 2) he has no discernible hope of winning, either by knockout or decision." What are the standards or ethics for street fighting?

---

*See Jeanne Gordon, "Teaching Kids to Negotiate," *Newsweek* (April 23, 1990), p. 65.

15

Duke It Out, Boys!

Nobody knows what really happened
Or why they started the fight
Or who was in the right.
But the little fellow was really scared.

Funny thing about it was—they were both scared.
The tough guy had that set of jaw broadcasting that
He would take on anyone.—
He couldn't bear to back down
And look like a caved-in macho man

Back down? Not on his life
Not in front of everybody
(It has happened to me and I knew they
        were both shaky and sick in the
        deep pit of their stomachs.)

How grateful they would feel
If someone intervened
With a rescue from this trap

What's the sense of slamming and punching
'Till the blood runs?
Instead of acting like sensible kids who know there's
A smarter way to get along.

If it's brute strength they want to worship,
They shouldn't waste their time around here.
They should take a look at the gorilla in the zoo.
Now that's real power!
He could take them all on—
        Splat! like a jelly donut stomp!
So much for brains and fights.

If they had real guts and courage,

They'd say,—"Let's talk this over and find a better way to settle."

Greta B. Lipson

 GA1417

Activities

- This poem speaks to the idiosyncracies and differences among siblings which is true of most families. Offspring from the same household often exhibit differences that are hard to explain. Each person, however, sees other family members critically and often regards them as being terribly flawed. Because there are so many differences among people, the variety within families should help prepare us to value the enriching diversity in school, community, and the greater world. In a written family portrait, how would you describe the similarities and differences among you? What personality characteristics do you or other family members have that are unique or unusual?

- If you could be an only child, what would your life be like? Would it be somewhat better, boring, lonely, peaceful, or what? Imagine writing a journal entry which accounts for your time at home and on weekends as an only child. Or, if you are currently the only one at home, how would brothers or sisters change your life?

- In a drama group, role-play a discussion in the house with all the siblings. Capture everyone's place in the pecking order. Decide on a topic which you believe is often a source of conflict. For example: Imagine discussing choices for activities for a holiday weekend and the possibilities of family time together. Will it be a swimming day, a game of baseball, a picnic, or a spin around the roller rink? Or perhaps the discussion will be as simple as deciding how the kids will divide the clean-up responsibilities after a family party! What is the outcome? Whose wishes prevail?

- What makes you proud of your siblings (even though you may hate to admit it)?

GA1417

We Are Three Brothers

We are three brothers
Not one of us alike
Except that two of us are slobs
And I'm the neatest dude.

    "You're crazy clean!" said one to the other
    As the houseflies circled overhead.
    I fell to the floor disbelieving.

They are sightless in the face of garbage
They are unperturbed by messes, scraps of leftover food,
Old exotic discards from turned out pockets
Tacky T-shirts, paperbacks, comics and broken drumsticks.

But they do have precious artifacts banked
In the archives of our house:
    A squirrel's tail in a drawer
    Small Match Box® metal cars from England
    An odoriferous ant farm
    A once puked-on quilt of synthetic manufacture
    (turned jarring orange from the upchuck of a sour stomach)
    A gutted clock whose Westminster-entrails still chime the time.

They are a mess these other two.
My mother in her forgiving tone says,
"They are personally clean. They shower every day."

They are awful! But together we are wonderful!
A skylight from the universe pours in and blesses our curiosity,
And bathes our brains and souls in lustrous light.

    Greta B. Lipson

GA1417

Activities

- People have always been concerned about the decline of the language, especially as it is spoken and written by young people. Language is a changing, dynamic form which responds to the culture. But given this fact, there remains an expressed concern by teachers, parents, and those in business who hear a general deterioration in speech. A person expresses this view in an "Op Ed" article in the *Daily Bugle.* Respond to the writer. Explain why you agree or disagree with the writer's opinion. Is it an accurate picture?

- Language is power. Language defines who you are. The ability to communicate effectively is part of your public image and the impression you make. There are expectations about the use of language as it is spoken by people at home, in school, in the marketplace, and in professional situations. Choose a particular profession for a role play "Language Cameo." Perform a spontaneous scene in the doctor's office wherein the physician comes across with unexpected language: "Hey dude, what's cookin'? You don't look like no mega-stud to me today. If you want it straight–I think you're a burned out dweeb." Reverse roles in other situations with adults who are supposed to be language role models. What's wrong with the picture? How does it make you feel?

- List as many current slang words and terms as you can and define them. Award a prize for the longest list and the best definitions. If you want to borrow from the past, your historical savvy is welcome, but you must be able to define the terms *cool, hip, awesome, waistoid, technoid, bad, cat, nerd, wuss,* and more! How does your slang keep outsiders out?

- Cut out a short human interest story from the newspaper that you believe is strange or very interesting. Read it until you know it well. Tell the story to the class in your own words, and try to keep your delivery smooth. Were there any problems with this speaking assignment? What were they? How can you improve your presentation?

Teen Speak

Like dude
Like man
Like find the meaning if you can

She goes
He goes
Translate it if you understand

Ya know, ya know
Ya know in every phrase
For sure,
Ya know
We hear it every place.

You're bad
You're good
Now get out of my face!

So lighten up
And cool it spaz
You're awesome and unreal
If you can't figure all this out
Don't make it such a deal.

Pretend that you are not a dweeb,
A simp, a wimp, or nerd
Just listen up the best you can
To every far-out word

It's context that'll clue you in
To the hippest of locutions
Just groove it, move it, all around
And reach your own conclusions.

                          Greta B. Lipson

LiKE TO-Tally
RĀD!
awesome

We hope
The harshness
Doesn't give offense.
The words
To some
Do truly make some sense.
(With apologies to Alexander Pope, turning in his grave)
Scurrilously quoted from *An Essay on Criticism*

17A

Activities

- This poem addresses the issue of parents giving teens mixed messages about behavior and expectations. For good measure parents also throw in a multitude of rules which are subject to change depending upon the circumstances. If you were asked to prepare a conspicuous chart for everyone in your household that was entitled "Rules of the Management," what would it look like? If there are rules on your list that may send contradictory signals, indicate them with some short phrase such as, "sometimes" or "now and then."

- If you were in your parents' position, what would you do about establishing rules for the family, discussing them, enforcing them, and helping everyone to understand the need or reasons for some guidelines. As a parent, would you feel that there are some absolutely inflexible rules that are not open to discussion? In a class discussion, determine some of the most common rules shared by households.

- Some parental criticism of behavior falls into two groups. Either you are too young to do something–or you are too old to do something (such as torment your brother or sister). Make two lists with the following headings:

    I AM TOO YOUNG TO   I AM TOO OLD TO

- Divide into groups and plan "role reversal" skits to present to the class. Decide on a single problem or source of conflict you have experienced. One of you will be the parent and one will be the adolescent. In a five-minute skit, try to get to the heart of the problem as each person makes his position clear. Discuss what you observed during each skit. Is right or wrong easily defined, or does it depend upon the adult's or child's point of view?

GA1417

Parents Are Confusing

You're too old for this
You're too young for that
It's conflicting, confusing
A dangerous trap!

Be a mother to your sister
Be a sister to your brother
Be a warm and loving person
To a multitude of others.

Get your elbows off the table
Keep your footsies on the floor
Finish food that's on your platter
Before you ask for more.

Don't interrupt a speaker
Never contradict a parent
Don't give the bad impression
That your manners are quite errant.

Always tell the truth,
But hurting feelings is forbidden
Be honest and revealing
But white lies will be forgiven.

Be sensible when making friends
Screen out the saints and sinners
(The trouble is, we don't agree
On which friends are the winners!)

The list of rules goes on at length
And so it will behoove you
To try your best to understand
So then we can improve you!

Greta B. Lipson

GA1417

Activities

- The title of the poem "Bywords" includes proverbs, cliches, and familiar sayings which are symbolic shortcuts to communicating some observations about life. You may or may not accept their quaint wisdom as being true, but these assorted nuggets have been around for a very long time. The term *scenario* means "an outline for a play, a movie, or an opera which includes scenes and characters." These sayings evoke an instant scenario or picture in the mind. The impression is made without a long discourse on the topic. A good example of this is "The grass is always greener on the other side." What instant picture comes to mind? Of the thirty-two choices in the poem, select five sayings and explain them in your own words.

- If you review these sayings long enough, you will find some that contradict one another. "Too many cooks spoil the broth" and "Two heads are better than one" are a good example. What other contradictions can you find? Is there one saying that you absolutely cannot figure out? Ask the class for help.

- Try to invent one or more sayings that have the old-fashioned quality of an authentic proverb. Ask members of the class to explain the message behind your proverb. Did your proverb express what you were trying to say, or did someone in the class give it a meaning that made it even more effective?

- With regard to people and language, do you agree that "Still waters run deep"? Do you believe that someone who never opens his/her mouth is the strong, silent type who has a deep personality? Or does it give you a pain in the neck when you can't get more than two words out of a person in a conversation? Argue with this proverb or any other saying in the poem. Support your point of view. (For a funny treatment of the strong/silent theme, read a review or a synopsis in your library about Jerzy Kosinski's novel *Being There*. What is the message about people who talk very little?)

19

GA1417

Bywords

She just fell off the turnip truck
A stitch in time saves nine
A bird in the hand is worth two in the bush
He stopped right on a dime.

Birds of a feather flock together
All that glitters is not gold
Grass is greener on the other side
Starve a fever–feed a cold.

Too many cooks spoil the broth
Let sleeping dogs lie
Don't count your chickens before they hatch
Said the spider to the fly.

Folks in glass houses shouldn't throw stones
Look before you leap
The squeaky wheel gets the grease
Still waters do run deep.

Every cloud has a silver lining
Never beat a dead horse
Take the tiger by the tail
But we must stay the course.

Beauty is only skin deep
Pure as the driven snow
The pen is mightier than the sword
You reap as you shall sow.

Little strokes fell great oaks
She really takes the cake
Dead men tell no tales, and
Good things come to those who wait.

Life is just a bowl of cherries
One hand washes the other
That's the way the cookie crumbles
One good turn deserves another.

Greta B. Lipson

GA1417

Activities

• Hair makes a statement. It is associated with youth, sexuality, virility, and strength. In history and literature, long hair has often had an androgynous* quality. The length and style of hair and its relative masculine or feminine look depend upon the popular culture of the time. Contribute to a class time line of hairstyles: braids, flips, dreadlocks, mohawk, high tops, chignon, ponytail, pageboy, pompadour, etc. Include illustrations drawn from your memory and from research.

• Hair is a vehicle for self-expression. One may adopt the style of the peer group (which may or may not be unconventional). One may subscribe to the norms of society with its vast range of what is considered normal. Strangely, hair may be used to shock as with the angry "skin heads" whose appearance is an immediate clue to their social posture. It announces something about the wearer as do the bizarre styles of the punkers with bright orange or green hair, mohawks, or whatever else is designed to unsettle the observer. Sketch a picture of the most outrageous hairstyle you have ever seen in modern times or in history. An all-time favorite is the wavy, curly wig worn by men in the French court of Louis XIV (1638-1715). Many were purported to be crawling with head lice.

• In mythology, hair is also a source of interest. You may know about Medusa who had hair of snakes or Lady Godiva, the eleventh century noblewoman of Coventry, England, who rode a horse naked through the streets with only her hair to protect her modesty. She was protesting an unfair tax! Put together a hair book. Give it a humorous name. Collect stories and myths which include hair as an important part of the story, such as Rapunzel and Medusa. Remember the story of Samson in the Old Testament, whose great strength lay in his uncut hair!

• Hair has a sensual rhythm and is a medium for theatrics and drama. It is central to the presentation of personality in our culture as evidenced by rock singers and other theatrical types. The preoccupation with grooming hair has a ritualistic aspect to it for adolescents. Combing one's hair, which can be a constant activity for some, is almost like a soothing balm for anxiety. Imagine you (or a group of students) work as high-powered copy writers for an advertising agency. Launch an advertising hair campaign to sell whatever hair products you choose. Use all the insights you have gained about people and their hair.

---

*Androgynous: having the qualities of both male and female

GA1417

I Worship at the Altar of Hair

High and curly
wavy, swirly
Long and short and fluffy poo

Kinky, springy
Straight and stringy
Thick and thin and bleached so true

Permanente–elegante
Dyed and fried
And conked all through

Braided, mohawked,
Scalped and frazzled
Tell the world that I love you.

Brains and soul may tell a story
But hair is still my crowning glory!
Comb it
Brush it
Clip it
Puff it
Mousse and tease it
Dunk and squeeze it

How about a nice shampoo?

Greta B. Lipson

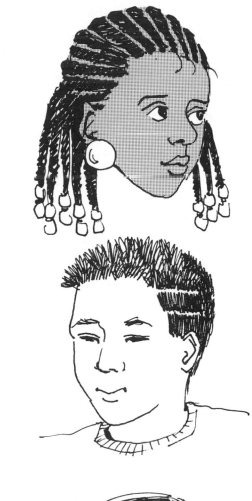

GA1417

Activities

- In this poem the older sister is talking about her younger sister with mixed feelings. On the one hand, she is annoyed by little sister and on the other, she admires her—sometimes grudgingly. There is a wonderful word that describes these conflicting feelings which take place at the same time. That word is *ambivalence*. If we are honest, we must admit that we have had ambivalent feelings toward friends, family members, teachers, and other people and things. What condition, person, or situation generates ambivalent feelings in you? Write a brief account of an incident in which you recognized this personal response. Did you understand it or was it another one of life's mysteries. Explain.

- What makes some sisters unfriendly toward one another? What would make some brothers unfriendly? What outside influences create this condition? How do you think family life changes when there are all boys or all girls in a family? If you wanted to change a sour relationship with your siblings to a good relationship, what could be done to help bring it about?

- Role-play a family discussion in which you have some specific complaints about your sister or brother. The adults in the family are present as you all sit down to discuss the problem. Set the time and place for the meeting. Establish guidelines so that everyone who has something to say can express it without any interruptions. To prevent hogging the discussion, set a timer in the room so that even the most talkative one knows when it's time to yield the floor. Ask the class to listen, take notes, and express their opinions after the discussion.

- Write a diary entry entitled "The Best Day I Ever Spent with My Brother/Sister!"

Sissy Poo

I love my sister
Though she's a thorn in my side.

I'm the oldest and we don't look alike
But the lady down the street keeps asking,
    "Are you sure you're not twins?"
And secretly I'm pleased.

Sissy Poo is smart, but I won't let her know I know.
She's popular and cute (and what could be more obnoxious)?

Sometimes when I'm feeling good, I say,
    "With your face and my personality we could wow them in Hollywood!"

When she was really little and I would be in the living room
    with a boyfriend and it would be dusk–
    She would come in and shine a flashlight on us.

And I would holler, "Get out you little twit."
But my father, of course, said it was harmless fun.

Sissy Poo and I have decided that if we weren't so much alike
it would be dynamite!
    She would be good in math and science,
    and I would be good in art and English
And then we would make a powerhouse team.

But we do anyway!
Did I say I love my sister?

Greta B. Lipson

GA1417

Activities

- Without looking in the dictionary, have everyone try to define the word *intelligence*. Write on a piece of paper to be handed in and read aloud to the class. After a sampling of the definitions have been read, the class should try to decide on a reasonable definition of the word. What problems are there in arriving at a definition? Is the word easy to define? Why or why not?

- In this poem our unnamed hero considers himself to be dumb. Wally, he believes, is very smart because "the brain" doesn't suffer over homework and everything seems to come so easily. What questions would you personally ask to determine just how smart Wally may be? Without any more information than the poem provides, write a character sketch of "Wally, the Brain."

- When you have read enough definitions of *intelligence,* you will probably conclude that intelligence can be a part of a very wide range of talents, abilities, interests, and assorted mysterious human factors. It is not just one single quality. Rarely is there someone who is good at everything. And besides, it isn't realistic to want to be. Our self-critical hero must have had some skills, otherwise how could he have grown up to be Wally's boss. With a class partner, discuss the reasons for our hero's success. In the form of a brief oral report, reveal more insights about him which you and your partner have deduced. You may feel forced to account for his smarts in ways you have never thought of before. Example: What role does motivation play in his personal success? Is there more than one analysis in class that seems realistic? If it helps your presentation, give our hero a name.

- Think about this: If you get very nervous and apprehensive about a test, even though you know your subject matter, what is likely to happen? What does school-work stress do to you?

- If you had a chance to write an editorial in the school paper regarding "homework reform" and felt comfortable about expressing your opinion without being punished, as a responsible student, what would you say?

GA1417

Homework

Wally was a smart kid; Wally was a brain
Wally did his homework and didn't even strain

I went to Wally's house to get a little help
He tried his best and then he said I'd have to help myself

Wally came to my house, inviting me to start
He tried to help me learn the stuff, though I'm not very smart

I went to Wally's house to fill up my poor brain
But all the hours Wally worked seemed to be in vain

Wally was my tutor; it didn't make him glad
The trouble I was having made me very sad

Wally ran away from me—he thought I was a bore
He didn't seem to understand that I would study more.

I went to Wally's house to ask him why he fled
He picked up a textbook and hit me in the head!

Wally is a grown-up now—but he is at a loss
'Cause Wally's life has changed a lot since I am Wally's boss!

Greta B. Lipson

GA1417

Activities

- Most people are ordinary looking, but we are beset on all sides by visions of beautiful women, handsome men, gorgeous children, and even good looking pets. What is visible to the eye is considered to be a standard of excellence. There is little or no emphasis on the internal qualities of people that are hardly measurable by physical appearance. Describe a person you have known who, at first glance, was unattractive but had a knockout personality or other wonderful qualities. After a while, you were so impressed with the outstanding attributes of this person that you were only conscious of his/her positive characteristics.

- The media reinforces a superficial standard of beauty which is defined by the culture. Media images are a constant daily reminder that we are never quite attractive enough to win the gifts of the gods who would reward us with happiness and good fortune if we really were better in all ways. Write some advertisements to be performed by TV and radio personalities that let you know emphatically that you need their product to improve yourself.

- Demonstrate the ways in which appearances may be deceiving. Each student will cut out a newspaper or magazine picture of a person of any age, sex or appearance. Mount the picture on construction paper. Include a short biographical sketch on the back. Pass the pictures around to class members. Do not look on the back! The class will speculate about who the people are, what each does for a living, identify their hobbies and more. While writing the biographical sketches, think positively, think negatively, think counter to stereotypes! What biographical information did the originator of the picture provide?

- Would our judgments about people be more sensible or accurate if we were sightless and not influenced by the physical aspects of a person? Explain your point of view.

GA1417

A Silk Purse or a Sow's Ear

Don't let yourself be influenced
By superficial things
I know you've heard this all before
It has the same old ring.

Good looks you fall for madly
May mask a real phoney
And everything about the guy (gal)
Could be full of baloney!

So look beyond the muscle
Look beyond the flair
Look beyond the cutesy nose
Look beyond the hair.

Ignore the popularity
Ignore the stylish clothes
Ignore the herd-bound attitudes
And look beyond the pose.

Look inside a person
Give it your best try
'Cause the quality of people
Is not measured by the eye.

Greta B. Lipson

23A

Activities

- A first job is similar to first days in school because of the great adjustments to be made. It represents a major step in a lifetime of work. Discuss basic skills that are needed to perform the job responsibilities for which you are likely to qualify at this time.

- Most people in a working lifetime will be answerable to a boss! Even a big, successful business person has a boss. She or he is responsible for following government regulations and city codes, for reporting to the Internal Revenue Service, and for running the business in an environmentally sound way. Who are the bosses of the people in your adult acquaintance? Start with your own teacher. Who is his or her boss, and who is that boss's boss? Illustrate this with a diagram on the chalkboard. (When students celebrate at graduation time and print banners declaring they will no longer be bossed by teachers, what surprises are in store for them?)

- Fast-food chains are the largest employer of young adults of school age. Some people believe that this kind of employment can be poor work experience for the following reasons: there is no way of climbing the ladder to promotion; the job requires few marketable skills; it may interfere with homework; long hours and fatigue may affect school attendance; the work schedule may eliminate the possibility of beneficial extracurricular activities. Write an opinion, pro or con. Is fast-food work experience a poor one? Follow up with a panel discussion.

- Many people who are talented and skilled will not have the advantage of attending college. Since it is always a good policy to plan ahead, what would the course of action be for someone who wants to enter the work force as a trained employee? What career information and counseling services are available in your school system or in other agencies? How does a person make the transition from school to work? Make this a class research project. Share the information about programs and resources for noncollege bound students.

I Work at Burger Barf

I don't have any training
Too young to have job skills
So I have to be satisfied
With a schedule that kills

I work at Ye Olde Burger Barf
Wear a goofy little hat
Am courteous to everyone
No back talk, and that's that!

Make time to do my schoolwork
No time to see my friends
Keep grilling dogs and burgers
'Till the week comes to an end.

The headline news for all of us
Is practical and wise
You need to train for decent pay
That comes as no surprise.

So finish school, old buddy
To get a decent job
'Cause there are better jobs than Burger Barf
Just dishing out the slop!

Greta B. Lipson

GA1417

Activities

• Owning a car is a very significant part of growing up. Many of the transitions that occur along the way from childhood to adulthood are not quite as dramatic as the moment of acquiring one's own automobile. Though there is no ritual to celebrate the event, it is one of the "rites of passage" in our society. Cars represent much more than convenient transportation for young adults, which suggests that there are social, psychological, and practical aspects to ownership. With class participation, record the specifics of the impact of an automobile in a teen's life. Use magic marker and a roll of butcher paper. Classify the items in whatever way you please. For example, a car means:

    ☐ Independence
    ☐ Adult responsibility and financial responsibility
    ☐ Power

• Write a description of the car of your dreams if money were no object. Give all the details of the make, model, color, accessories and the price of the car on the market today. To keep you in touch with reality, it would be interesting to actually consult a car dealer to determine the cost and the financing of payments. Report back to class. What do you think is meant by "sticker shock"?

• The owner in the poem says, "I never ever count the cost of other things I may have lost." What does this tell you about the cost and commitment of keeping the Tin Lizzie in working condition? Why would someone prefer a very old car to a more recent model?

• "Hot Dog" is a name for daredevils who cut in and out of traffic, endangering other drivers on the road. They cut perilously across lanes, passing on the right and left, not signalling, and driving at top speed. They gain a car length here and there–and tailgate if you don't accelerate fast enough to please them. They threaten life and limb, scare other drivers, and arrive at the same red light as everybody they passed. Write a descriptive scene starring a "Hot Dog" and wild ways on the road! (See page 64, "Fink of the Road.")

Cars and Sweet Thrills

Gramps named my car "Tin Lizzie"*
A relic of olden times
It rattles and shivers, this ancient flivver
And I'm proud to say it's mine.

Some sleight of hand—some welding tricks
Restored the moving parts
She's sparky, perky, strong and quirky
A car with a vintage heart.

I love to park my auto near
To shine and care for through the year
And I am filled with sheer delight
To spin around with her at night

I never ever count the cost
Of other things I may have lost

Oh Tin, Tin Lizzie
Oh Lizzie Tin
It has a sweet melodic ring
My super antique drive machine
An answer to my wildest dream.

Greta B. Lipson

*Henry Ford introduced the Model T Ford in 1908. It was referred to as the "Tin Lizzie" and was enthusiastically received by the public. It was manufactured in the Ford Factory in Highland Park, Michigan, and was a simple piece of machinery which home mechanics could easily repair. Research this car which was a remarkable breakthrough in automotive history.

GA1417

Activities

- Define the phrase "going with someone." Does it mean meeting one another in the hall when passing from class to class? Does it mean being together with other friends? Does it mean an exclusive relationship?

- There are some very comfortable aspects of knowing that there is someone who is there for you all the time, someone that you see at school, at social events, at the mall and in the neighborhood. Discuss the positive and negative aspects of this kind of relationship. How does it exclude all others?

- Sometimes you are going with someone only to discover that you are both interested in different things. Create a role-play skit to demonstrate just how difficult it can be when there is a conflict of interests. The two of you cannot agree on sports, dancing, eating, friends and other aspects of your life in and out of school. You are having a heated discussion over going to the homecoming game, dance, party, concert, poetry reading, debate, drama club, fencing match, art show, pizza fest, or state fair. How can incompatibility be solved or does it just get worse between two people?

- Imagine that there is an incredible dating service in your school, offering its services at no charge. The only requirement is that you must include a picture of yourself and provide the staff with an accurate description of your interests, your values, personality, likes, and dislikes. You must then describe specifically the kind of person you would like selected as your companion. In small groups organize this computer dating service, give it a name, and develop a questionnaire that will include all the data your dating office requires of its clients.

- The writer of the poem "Going with Someone" takes advantage of some Mother Goose rhymes and uses them as a parody for the fickleness and instability of boy/girl relationships. A parody is a piece of writing that copies or exaggerates another style of writing in a humorous way. Can you write a short parody of a song, poem, or prose piece and give it a twist? Look at Mother Goose for inspiration.

GA1417

Going with Someone

I love my boyfriend, that I do,
And Ginny says she loves him, too
But we both say
We fear someday
With some bad girl he'll run away

Little Miss Pink
Dressed in Blue
Danced last night
'Till 12 past two

Before she danced
She told me this,
"Your boyfriend loves me more than you.
    He promised me a big fat kiss."

Do you believe this saucy Miss?

****

I love my girlfriend, that I do
And Jimmy says he loves her, too
But we both say
We fear some day
With some bad boy she'll run away.

It finally happened by and by
When Georgie Porgie Puddin and Pie
Kissed my girl and made her cry.

She fell in love with him at once
This heartless, handsome, daring dunce

Do you believe this rotten runt?

Greta B. Lipson

GA1417

Activities

- In *The Teachers and Writers Handbook of Poetic Forms*, edited by Ron Padgett, published by Teachers and Writers Collaborative, 1987, there is a poetic form called "pantoum," pronounced pan-toom. The original pantoum was a Malayan form written in the fifteenth century. It was first described in the West in 1829 by Victor Hugo, the great French poet who wrote *The Hunchback of Notre Dame* and *Les Miserables*.

The form became popularized in America with the interest of another poet, John Ashbery. It became a poem of "indefinite" length, arranged along a pattern which used each line in the poem twice. Each stanza has four lines. The first line of the poem is the last.

In our poem "It's How You Play the Game," the first and second lines were used as the last line because both lines represent a single idiomatic expression. Happily there are no poetry police so there are times you are permitted such creative license!

The fascination of the form is that it has the quality of a puzzle whose parts appear and reappear to form an intriguing tapestry of words. You may always change some of the recurrent lines which do not please you as they are repeated in the body of the completed poem. Try this impressionistic exercise on your own. Everyone start out with the same two lines of this poem, or any other topic. Rhyme is optional. Good luck!

Pantoum

Line 1 _____

Line 2 _____

Line 3 _____

Line 4 _____

Line 5 (Use 2 above.) _____

Line 6 _____

Line 7 (Use 4 above.) _____

Line 8 _____

Line 9 (Use 6 on left.) _____

Line 10 _____

Line 11 (Use 8 on left.) _____

Line 12 _____

Line 13 (Use 10 above.) _____

Line 14 _____

Line 15 (Use 12 above.) _____

Line 16 _____

Continue on your own!

GA1417

It's How You Play the Game

1	It isn't whether you win or lose
2	It's how you play the game
3	It's not about personal glory
4	Not the search for public acclaim
5-2	It's how you play the game
6	Observe the motto with valor
7-4	Not the search for public acclaim
8	A loss is never a shame
9-6	Observe the motto with valor
10	The regal emblem of sport
11-8	A loss is never a shame
12	Inspire the pure of heart.
13-10	The regal emblem of sport
14	A lost game is only the start
15-12	Inspire the pure of heart
16	Be steadfast in team support.
17-14	A lost game is only the start
18	Then what is it all about
19-16	Be steadfast in team support
20	The infinite challenge of sport
21-18	Then what is it all about
22	The ultimate win is pride
23-20	The infinite challenge of sport
24	True spirit will always abide
25-22	The ultimate win is pride
26	The honor is yours to choose
27-24	True spirit will always abide
28-1	It isn't whether you win or lose
	It's how you play the game!

Greta B. Lipson

27A

Activities

- Probably the most damaging attitude toward poetry in the classroom is the notion that it has to rhyme, that it must be about something remote from the experience of ordinary people, and it must be obscure in its content and meaning. None of this is true! Talk to your school or neighborhood librarian and ask for modern poems for young adults that deal with sports, humor, adventure, working, rural life, city life and anything which reflects our world presently. Put together a bibliography of the poetry titles, authors, and the books from which they came. As a class, produce your own poetry bibliography of upbeat selections that speak to today's young people.

- In modern society poetry has become something of a lost art, though its less pure form is still experienced in popular culture in the form of song lyrics. Poetry dates back to ancient times and served as a form of entertainment and as a means of preserving history in the oral tradition. Instead of popping in a compact disc or videocassette or turning on the evening news, ancient peoples listened to poets and musicians for entertainment and information. People relied on the rhythm and cadence of poetry because it was much easier to remember lyrics in that form. Bring in the lyrics of your favorite song, copied on tagboard or on a large sheet of paper. Be prepared to analyze the meaning of the lyrics, line by line, in front of the class. Be specific about every line. Which phrases or sections do you not understand? Can anyone in the class speculate on the meaning?

- Find a poem which speaks to you very strongly because it witnesses for you or expresses your personal point of view. Or select any poem which captivates you. Indicate in writing why the poem attracted your interest. Neither you nor the poem has to be profound! Most importantly, make sure you truly understand it! Copy the poem, including the author, and hand it in to the "Poetry Committee." The group will organize the poems and schedule a poetry reading at the end of each week, including just two or three people at a time. If you would like your poem read by someone else, you may indicate that on your paper. Your selection may be modern or traditional, as long as it is your special choice!

28

Poetry Pain

Oh give me a poem where the words aren't moaning
Where emotions don't sag and the poet's not groaning
Where ideas are clear and not hiding out
In sullen allusions and phrases that pout

Give me a poem that probes like a thistle
With color and power—with muscle and gristle
Use words that are dazzling with vigor and verve
With the clearness and brilliance a poem deserves

Oh save me from poems I don't understand
So mystic and bleak, so pallid and bland.
Don't bore with mysterious words I deplore
Use honest and tough words I cannot ignore.

Greta B. Lipson

28A

GA1417

Activities

- When you care about someone, it means that you take the chance of loss or rejection. But most of us are willing to take the risk. Many questions begin to arise following a breakup: could it have been avoided; was there another person in the picture; was the magic gone; were you at fault? Putting events in their proper perspective enables a person to recover. For these reasons it can be helpful to have the advice of people who have had a similar experience. Organize a staff to produce an advice column. Give the column a catchy name to attract reader interest. Encourage people with romantic problems to seek advice from the "heartbreak" columnist by writing anonymous letters describing problems of themselves or others. Review the letters first and select a representative number to be read to the class for helpful, responsive solutions.

- This poem is directed at the inevitability of loss and grief throughout life. The loss of friends, family members, or pets creates pain–whether through fate or the natural course of events. And we are obliged to deal with these occurrences. The surprise ending of this poem seems to be a joke, but parting–from anyone or anything–can be shattering. The ways in which we resolve our grief, or deny it, or come to accept it vary from person to person. Have you had some experience with loss that you could express? Write a nonrhyming poem, taking your lead from the style of "Breaking Up." Let the feelings and impressions flow as you write in the most lyrical language you find inside.

- Role-play a situation where a peer counselor, in a private session, is helping another student. They are dealing with the unhappiness of a broken friendship. This time the counselor is a very good listener who does not give advice but reflects on the difficulty of the experience. As the student sorts out his/her feelings, the counselor gives the student space and silence. As a member of the audience, do you prefer the good listener who gives a sad person permission to feel bad or do you prefer an advice giver? Following the role play, discuss or write your impressions of which approach would be the best for you.

GA1417

Breaking Up

Thoughts of you are leaden chunks lodged in my chest
     near my faltering heart.
How can it be that your absence gives me physical pain and
     oppresses every thought throughout my day?
Reviewing our times together I wonder why you didn't care enough
     to stay.
Should I have been more attentive, when you needed me?
Did I fail you? Was I less than you wanted me to be?
Or was there someone else—better perhaps—more loving—
     someone who laughed when you were funny—more patient with
     your changing moods?

There was a compelling magic between us. We didn't need words.
Do you recall our harsh encounters and the joy of sweet reunion?

Reminded of your absence and my loss—
     unanswered questions never cease.
They give me so much grief.

Your eyes were warmest topaz.
And now you're gone.

Doggie, please come home!

    Greta B. Lipson

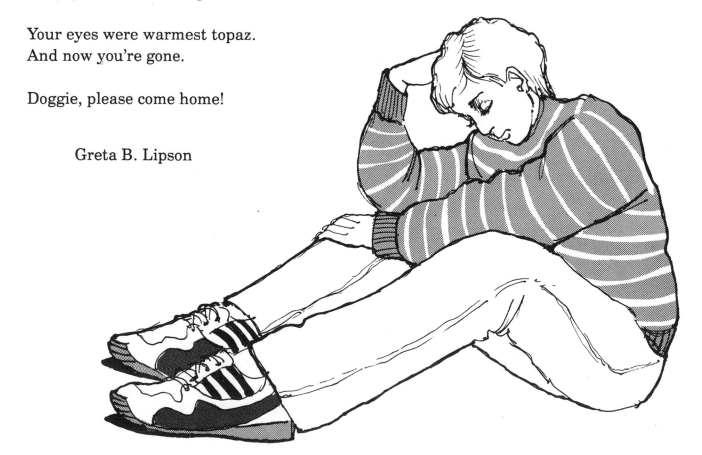

GA1417

Activities

- Once upon a time there was a first grade classroom in Anytown, USA. It was at the end of the school day and the children were happily celebrating a pupil's birthday. All of a sudden the door opened and Mr. Grouch, the neighborhood curmudgeon, stomped in uninvited. Everyone gasped. It was very rude to come in without knocking and interrupt the business of the classroom. But the teacher, Ms. Friendly, was very courteous as she turned to Mr. Grouch and asked, "How can I help you?"

"You" he said, pointing an accusing finger at the teacher, "are wasting tax payers' money by celebrating birthdays, and singing songs about them, and eating goodies during school hours. You should be doing important things for your pupils!"

The class was silent as they waited for Ms. Friendly's response. Every single heart in the room beat as one in sympathy for her ordeal, because she had to find an answer. Everybody knows that celebrating birthdays is the thing to do! How can you explain the answer to something so obvious? Everybody understands a birthday celebration without any formal instruction! How could he ask such a dumb question?

Put yourself in the teacher's place and answer Mr. Grouch's question. Consider carefully your feelings about:

- ☐ your birthday
- ☐ the uniqueness of every single human being
- ☐ the value of each of us
- ☐ the difference that one person can make in the world
- ☐ the potential of each individual
- ☐ the contribution, large or small, each of us hopes to make
- ☐ the collective influence of a good society
- ☐ the celebration and miracle of human life

- If you agree with Mr. Grouch and want to be heard, use the above ideas to argue his point of view.

Birthday Praise

Your birthday this year
Is a regal affair
So do up your face,
Your bod and your hair.

Pull out the stops
Wear a smile that is bright
And you'll get a cake
That's a layered delight!

Your guests will arrive
You'll think it's a dream
The right folks will come
They're the "Cream della Cream."

All shouting at once
They'll be singing your praises
"You're gorgeous and smart,"
In swell birthday phrases.

Accept admiration
Don't burst their sweet bubble
Be gracious for now
And don't make no trouble.

Smile and say, "Thank you,"
To your fans, one and all
Make the most of your day
Have a great birthday ball.

Greta B. Lipson

30A

Activities

- The shopping mall has assumed its own distinctive place as a gathering center for teens. It was announced on "The Weekend Edition" of National Public Radio (WDET, Detroit, Sunday, October 28, 1990) that *The Orange County Register*, a California newspaper, now has a regular mall beat. It is the first newspaper of its kind to assign a reporter (Janet Lowe) to cover the mall news. It is expected that other local newspapers will follow with similar columns. As an authentic maller what kinds of items of interest do you think occur at the mall and what would be interesting for readers? Write your own human interest mall feature. What will the name of your regular column be?

- A fantasy shared by many people is one that allows us to be locked up alone–after hours–in a department store with full freedom to roam around. You can try on great clothes, test sports equipment, find your way to the bakery and candy departments, and have an all 'round wonderful time! Write a paragraph describing what you think you would do in that situation. Locate the book *Secrets of the Shopping Mall* by Richard Peck, © 1979, Dell Publishing Co. Before reading it, speculate on what you think those secrets may be.

- "Kid purchasing power" is important in the marketplace! Business people who sell and advertise products must learn as much about adolescent life, values, styles, tastes, and preferences as they are able to. Advertisers know that the peer group has a strong influence on the clothing that is worn, the games that are popular, the food that is preferred, the music listened to, and countless other factors that mean big business! Imagine that you are a psychologist working in the field of market research. Act out a skit in which you are in the mall with your trusty clipboard and are interviewing young passersby. Ask questions about shampoo, cosmetics, games, jeans, sporting goods, or any other items important to adolescents. What are your conclusions?

The Mall

The mall, the mall,
A place for all
The guys and dolls
Who love the mall.

It's independence hall for us
No parents near to make a fuss

Unload the servitude of school
Enjoy the easy cooler rules!

Hang out and see what's comin' down.
Keep track of all the kids in town.

A smorgasbord of junk for treats
No flak when we wolf down our eats

The glitter, the glamour, the sparkle of lights
The action and air is charged and is bright

The energy's high for people suburban
The kicks are the same for the folks who are urban

There's comfort in groups
There's warmth in a gaggle
Dress to the nines*–you're not welcome bedraggled!

The mall, the mall,
It's paradise
Where gals are cute
and guys are spice!

Greta B. Lipson

---

*See *Dictionary of Cliches*, Facts on File, 1985, New York. The term *dressed to the nines* goes back to Revolutionary times. Originally *to the eyne* meant, to the eye–or one who dressed to please the eye, or dressed to perfection.

GA1417

Activities

• Create an ongoing, alphabetical, classroom list on a role of butcher paper of authentic "ologys" and another list of made-up "ologys." Students may add contributions in magic marker. How long will the list grow?

anthropology
archeology
astrology
audiology
biology
chronology
craniology
ecology
entomology
eschatology
etymology
garbology
gemology
geneology
geology
histology
immunology
meteorology
microbiology
neology
neurology
oncology
otolaryngology
pathology
pharmacology
phrenology
physiology
psychology
sarcology
scatology
sociology
tautology
technology
theology
urbanology
urology
virology
zoology

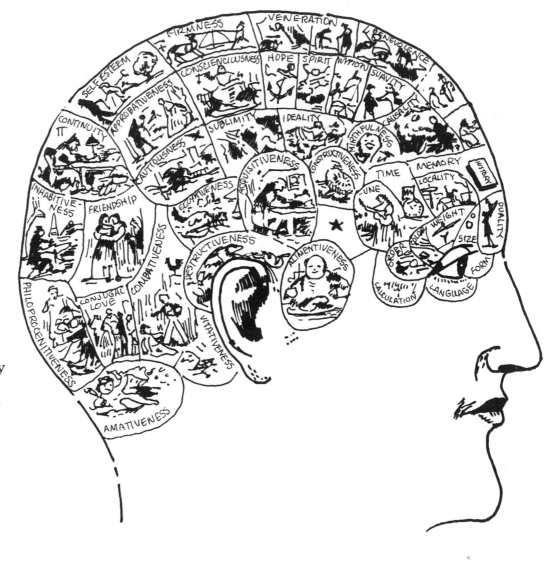

GA1417

Brainology

Do you know about stupology?
Or the star who loves beautology
Do you know a guy with ego-ology
Or a dog who studies barkology
Or our baby who does cryology
Or a pilot who knows flyology
Or a kid whose career is smartology
Or the sneak who practices smarmology
Have you seen the tough who takes muscleology
Or the chef who thrives on cookology
Or the ratty kid who does rottenology
Or the fat kid who understands eatology
Or the dad who majors in nagology
Or the sport who's freaked with jockology
Or the teacher who's an expert in bore-ology
Or the big mouth who suffers from mouthology
Or the liar who practices fibology
Or my kid brother who was born with pestology
Or the flea brain who studies bubbleology
Or the big shot who is expert at bullology?

Greta B. Lipson

Activities

- In poetry, the author is able to communicate strong statements, emotions, and attitudes without editorializing or explaining. The words do it all. They are the poem. They are the poet. The words stand as a collection of impressions which speak for the feelings of the writer. Reading or writing a poem can be like holding the reflective wonders of a kaleidoscope up to the eye. You turn it to see the variegated streaks of brilliant color and patterns. If you were to choose one topic for a poem and assign it to an infinite number of writers, you would get back an infinite number of poems. There isn't a right way or a wrong way. There isn't one correct form in the design of a poem. Here is a way to try it out: Write a poem about your parents or an important adult in your life. It may rhyme or not rhyme according to your choice (though nonrhyming poems allow for more expression with no forced, nonsense rhyme words).

- Now try using the form of the poem "Parental Triolet." The result is surprising because the poem almost works itself out like a crossword puzzle. Your topic will be the same as above. Copy the poem, number the lines, and indicate the rhyme scheme. Here is the pattern for a triolet which has eight lines with eight syllables each.

    ☐ Line 1-4-7, use the same lines
    ☐ Line 2-8, use the same lines

    The rhyme scheme is abaaabab.

- The poem "Parental Triolet" deals with a fact of life for teenagers. Adolescence is a time when teens begin to move away from the nuclear family and try to establish their own identity. Because of this developmental change, there are many sensitive issues to deal with. One of these issues (as indicated in the poem) is not wanting to appear to be a dependent child any longer–particularly in public. If you had to explain this situation to someone and wanted them to understand that you still loved your parents, what would you say?

GA1417

*Parental Triolet**

Being with parents isn't cool.

It's just because it looks all wrong.

It's very much a rigid rule.

Being with parents isn't cool.

Don't want to look like little fools!

With folks is not where we belong.

Being with parents isn't cool.

It's just because it looks all wrong.

Greta B. Lipson

---

*Triolet: A poem or stanza having eight lines of eight syllables each. Line one is repeated in lines four and seven. The second line is repeated in line eight. The rhyme scheme is abaaabab.

GA1417

Activities

- Denotation and connotation are interesting concepts because they are a factor in the decision about what words you will use in writing or speaking. The denotation of a word means the precise definition of the word as listed in the dictionary. The connotation of a word is the feeling or emotion that is stimulated by the word. Such words as *foreigner, ambitious, right wing, liberal, explicit, atheist* evoke a quick reaction in the minds of many people. When you hear the word *attitude*, what does it conjure up for you? First look up the dictionary definition (denotation) and then explain the connotation of that word for you as it relates to the mood of the poem.

- If a trained psychologist told you that a person with an attitude is really very insecure, lacking in confidence, and just trying to cover up for poor feelings of personal worth, how could you explain that in a convincing way to someone who was trying to understand this behavior. Write out your response with the starting sentence: "The real reason behind this behavior is..." Do you agree or disagree with the psychologist?

- Some words (such as *attitude*) may carry an offensive message. Because of the emotional impact of these harsh expressions other words are sometimes substituted. The substitute or more agreeable words are called "euphemisms." This illustrates the power of language which can make us uncomfortable or put us at ease–though the meaning of a word may be clear to us no matter how we mask it. A popular example is "passed away" which means someone has died. Euphemisms may be positive or negative. The positive form makes things seem grander and more important: a garbage collector becomes a "sanitary engineer," an undertaker becomes a "mortician," a janitor becomes a "custodian." Negative forms of euphemisms tend to diminish or be insulting: an articulate person becomes a "big mouth," a concerned parent becomes an "hysteric," a hearty eater becomes a "pig." *How many euphemisms can you find in your daily paper? Try the editorial section for starts.

---

* See *A Dictionary of Euphemisms and Other Doubletalk* by Hugh Rawson, Crown Publishers, Inc., New York, 1981.

An Attitude

Do me a favor and look me in the eye
Then get yourself together and tell me why–
You've got an attitude

You know you're not a favorite
And you can't say why.
But our entire class
Could give it a try!

You've got an attitude we call "horrific"
You anger everyone you talk to
And we'll be specific

You scoff and you smirk
You scorn and you sneer
You snub with disdain
And demean with a jeer
Your contempt is a pain
We suggest you refrain
From your attitude.

The chip on your shoulder
Is most detrimental
If you want to reform
Here's advice elemental

Change if you can
Put a smile on your face
The hostile and sullen
Is yours to erase.

When your attitude's gone
And good cheer's in its place
Maybe then–if you're lucky
We'll like you!

Greta B. Lipson

GA1417

Activities

• Almost all of us have had the experience of trying to repress a huge laugh because it was inappropriate at the time. The effort to keep it under control seems to compound the buildup of energy until the laugh grows and has a life of its own. Have you had a similar experience in school, in church, as a guest in someone's home, or during a serious presentation? Share that agonizing moment with the class.

• Laughter is a great release from tension. It helps us to stop taking ourselves so seriously; it is therapeutic; and it is the satisfying reward for humor. While we can't all be comedians it is possible to find a joke, a riddle, or an anecdote to deliver effectively to an audience. Find an appropriate selection that feels comfortable for you. (Good taste is your guideline. Exclude ridicule, ethnic jokes or off-color stories. You are always free to poke fun at yourself.) Read your selection over and over again until you have it mastered. Rehearse it out loud for a few victims at home, or even in front of the mirror. Some earnest practice, a sense of timing, and a little style will help put it over. Now you are ready to tell it to your class. You must be in front of the class for more than a few seconds. Stand straight, project that voice, keep up the volume, and slow down! Break a leg.

• For the Teacher:

What do you get when you cross an insomniac, a dyslexic, and an atheist?
Do you give up?

You get someone who stays up all night wondering if there really is a dog!

• Deliver a book talk on the funniest book you ever read. Organize your review in the form of a synopsis so that you do not spoil the entire story for the reader. You may want to read a passage from the book that was especially humorous. Make your listeners want to rush right out to find the book.

GA1417

The Captive Laugh

It started just like that
In front and not in back
Inspired by a gaffe
That happened in the class.

Laughter chuckled in my nose
And shot down to my toes
As I struggled in its throes
Disturbing my repose
       For I knew a crazy laugh
       Must not happen in this class.

It puffed out all my clothes
While trying to explode
It electrified my hair
I suppressed it then and there.

It demanded to get out
It dashed itself about
It banged against my ears
It flooded me with tears
It pushed against my teeth
It gave me no relief.

I fell upon the floor–
Kids opened up the door
I held my sides in pain
But my efforts were in vain.

I was abloat with bursting laughter
About to shake the rafters.
They rolled me to the office
Where our principal, the boss is.

All at once that laugh erupted
Uncorrupted–not abrupted!
In drowning waves of mirth
The dam had finally burst.
For the school it was a first
An implosion–a disaster–a most serious cataster
On the wacky scale of laughter
I had scored a hundred one!

Greta B. Lipson

GA1417

Activities

- True, we have no choice in the names that are given us by our parents. Before we judge them too harshly, it must be admitted that there is no way of knowing how well the name will fit the adult model of the cute little six-pound bundle when he/she grows to adulthood! In addition, the popularity of names is cyclical. In any given decade biblical names like John, Jacob, Sarah and Rebecca may be current only to make way later for Scott, Ashley, and Robin. But like it or not, names do suggest a wide variety of qualities and personalities. What adults have you encountered with names that simply do not fit. Why? Think about celebrities.

- What is the funniest name you have ever heard (excluding people in your school)? What do you think makes it funny?

- Write a paragraph about your feelings toward your own given (first) name and surname (last name). Do you prefer to be called by your nickname? What name do you believe would better suit your personality? If you were to become an actor and had to change your entire name to something really flashy, what would that name be?

- Do some library work and research the names of famous people. These personalities may be historical or from modern times. Find a name, male or female, that is really unusual! Make note of who and what your chosen personality was famous for. Write the name on a piece of paper entitled "What's My Line." Everyone will hand these in to the teacher to be collected and mixed in a container. Each student will pick a piece of paper, read the name silently, and write out a brief fictional biography of the famous person based solely upon the name. After each paper is read aloud, the originator will stand and give the true biographical information. Example: Sojourner Truth and Evel Knievel. Hint: Look in *The Almanac of Famous People.*

What's in a Name?

BERTHA

Brave Prince Charming in distress, as

Elegant as one could hope for in

Romantic dreams—fighting a losing battle

To a formidable and vicious dragon when all at once I slew the beast!

He turned to me with love, and he (sweet and grateful boy)

Asked me what my name was. God, how could you do this to me?

MY NAME

My mind conjures up visions of knights of

Yesteryear, when I am a warrior of

Noble bearing, as I storm the castle ramparts in gleaming

Armor, defeating powerful and aggressive adversaries!

Many have fallen to my sword even though my name is

Elmer—or perhaps, because of it!

Greta B. Lipson

GA1417

Activities

- The poem "Avoid Goo" is to be read from left to right, back and forth, following the dialogue that takes place (as if in a tennis match). The theme is that talk is cheap, particularly when it is not sincere or there is a hidden motive. It doesn't cost a thing to make flattering comments to someone. But it does exact a price to be a real friend through good times and bad. If you had to analyze the reasons for insincere behavior, what would you assume were the reasons in the mind of the flatterer? What is the motivation? What is the payoff?

- Trouble is an astonishing test of friendship. It can be a time when certain truths about your own feelings, in relation to others, are revealed to you as well. What is more astonishing is that some of the people you see on a daily basis, who seem to be closest to you, are not the ones you would go to in time of personal difficulty. If you were feeling down and needed support or advice, who would be the most likely peer you would contact? Write your answers and then respond to the following question: Why wouldn't you go to some of the people you hang out with? What does it tell you about your values and attitudes?

- Look up the definition of the word *flattery*. What makes flattery so difficult to resist? Role-play a situation in which the victim of the flattery is trying to keep the dialogue honest and is not falling for the irresistible compliments. For example:

    The Phoney: I have never in my life seen a performance as brilliant as yours in the school play!

    The Victim: Well, thank you for the kind words. But it sounds like you don't get around very much.

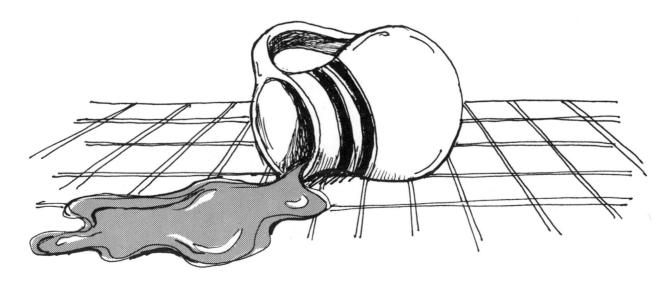

37

Avoid Goo

When ------------we
meet--------------face
to-----------------face
you----------------are
full----------------of
syrupy------------praise
but----------------when
it-----------------matters
you---------------are
never------------there
as----------------a
sincere-----------friend.

Greta B. Lipson

GA1417

Activities

- Alexander Pope was an English poet with enormous influence in literature. He was a master of satire and was the "literary dictator of his time." Examine the quote in the first stanza of this poem. If he were to say that to you today, face to face, you would think he was arrogant and a smart aleck besides. Try to paraphrase and explain his remark in your own words. (Satire: the use of sarcasm, ridicule and irony)

- Nobody believes that as a student you have to produce professional writing whenever you put pencil to paper. But such mean-spirited criticism as Mr. Pope's could discourage a student from even trying. What advice would you give to someone who wanted to write poetry (or prose) but was afraid of not being good enough and afraid of being called a fool besides?

- Many students get a brain block when they are expected to write in school. What are some of the reasons people have great trouble expressing themselves in writing? If you believe it has something to do with the topics assigned in class and it was within your power to assign some of your own ideas, what would they be? Develop a list of subjects which you believe could generate a good student response from reluctant writers.

- Donald Culross Peattie in *An Almanac for Moderns* said (more kindly than Alexander Pope), "A poet should always be hungry or have a lost love." What did he mean by that statement? Write your own pearl of wisdom about poets, starting in the same way, "A poet should always...." Try as often as you like to finish the quote. Which statements in class are the most interesting, the funniest, or the most profound? Have volunteers read their own quotable quotes to the class.

GA1417

Alexander Pope Was No Dope

"Sir, I admit your general rule,
That every poet is a fool:
But you yourself may serve to show it,
That every fool is not a poet."*

Though Alex Pope was not a dope
Don't let it rob you of all hope.
You may not be a fool or poet
But yield to sentiment—be verbal and show it!

It's healthy and sound to express an emotion
And poetry eases like soothing lotion
Though your efforts may seem a little bit rough
Just strut your lyrical sensitive stuff!

AFTERTHOUGHT:

(Al may write a hot epigram—
But we all don't think he's incredibly grand.
Besides his imperious classical stand
He's purported to have been an incurable ham.)

Greta B. Lipson

---

*Epigram by Alexander Pope (1688-1744).

GA1417

Activities

- Loss and change are universal issues for everyone. Early in life it is comforting to operate under the fantasy that the conditions that make life happy will stay the same. Unfortunately, change is entirely outside of our control. Through change we learn about the fragility of things which we may have previously taken for granted. We learn later to cherish the sweetest of those nurturing memories. Even the youngest of us has a favorite memory. What is yours? Write a cameo description which could be a journal entry. Include background information—your age, the place, and any other details that bring the memory to life.

- Consider the things you think you can control in your life and those you cannot control. Open the exercise to the entire class and make three columns on the chalkboard, with the headings **Control**, **No Control**, **Undecided**. Accept all suggestions; then discuss the category under which these events have been placed. What, if any, special problems do you encounter in attempting to categorize? Is there a solution to the problem or does it remain a difference of opinion?

- A very wise and philosophical prayer comes from the Alcoholics Anonymous organization: "God grant me the serenity to accept the things I cannot change, courage to change the things I can, and wisdom to know the difference." How could the wisdom of that prayer help anyone under any circumstances? Over a period of time, collect similar words of wisdom to live by; print them on banners and display them around your classroom. Remember to cite the source in detail.

- Within the framework of conditions you cannot change such as illness or tragedy, how do you think you can still exercise some control? (Answer: You can exercise control by the way you conduct yourself.)

- The poem "I Hate Change" is a pantoum, which is a fifteenth-century Malayan poetic form. It uses every line twice in a designated format. Using seven verses, the first line of the poem becomes the last line of the poem. The lines of this non-rhyming poem on the opposite page have been numbered as a guide to the pattern. See page 27, "It's How You Play the Game," for complete directions. Try it.*

---

*Ron Padgett, editor, *The Teachers and Writers Handbook of Poetic Forms*, copyright 1987. Teachers and Writers Collaborative, New York.

I Hate Change

1	Don't tell me what I cannot bear
2	All things and people change
3	Some feel, in this, no loss at all
4	For me there's desperate pain.
5-2	All things and people change
6	No, nothing stays the same
7-4	For me there's desperate pain
8	It rends my soul to face.
9-6	No, nothing stays the same
10	The earth beneath me shifts
11-8	It rends my soul to face
12	The cruelty of change.
13-10	The earth beneath me shifts
14	As distant voices fade
15-12	The cruelty of change
16	Sweet laughter falls away.
17-14	As distant voices fade
18	Where will the faces go
19-16	Sweet laughter falls away
20	No memory is safe.
21-18	Where will the faces go
22	I yearn to hold them close
23-20	No memory is safe
24	Will life just fade away?
25-22	I yearn to hold them close
26	On evanescent air
27-24	Will life just fade away?
28-1	Don't tell me what I cannot bear.

Greta B. Lipson

39A

GA1417

Activities

- The notion of boredom is said to have been invented (or discovered) by an Englishman, Earl Carlisle, in 1768. He was the first person to use the word *bore* as a transitive verb. As could be expected, he and his countrymen blamed this hideous condition on the French by calling it "the French bore." By 1818 the scourge of boredom was firmly entrenched—and to be avoided at all costs.* Write an article for a newspaper that might have existed in those times with a complete account of the new, alarming "discovery" called boredom. Name the newspaper and the section in which it will appear. Is it a disease? Are there any known antidotes?

- Can you recall the most monumentally boring experience you have ever endured? Write a description of the situation in full detail. How did it happen to you? How long did it last? How did you escape the monotony (in your mind)?

- Organize small committees with the assigned purpose of compiling an "Anti-boredom Summertime Activity Handbook." Think of places to go and things to do for you, your friends, and members of the family. Make a careful search of your daily newspaper. Look for those feature sections having various headings such as family fun, sports, free summer concerts, swimming, roller rinks, art festivals, greenhouse and floral exhibits, boat shows, camping shows, museums, the aquarium, the zoo, etc. Organize the information according to those that are free of charge and those that charge admission. As an important addition include volunteer activities that could broaden your horizons and make a genuine contribution to the community in which you live. You may also include suggestions for part-time jobs or any other items of interest to students. The production of this handbook could be of genuine value to many inactive kids in the summer.

---

*Wayne C. Booth, *The Vocation of a Teacher: Rhetorical Occasions, 1967-1988*, The University of Chicago.
See also: "Noted with Pleasure," New York Times Book Review, January 20, 1991.

40   GA1417

Summer Boredom

School is out
Boredom's in
Wimping around
Is a mortal sin
Nothin' to do
No one to see
Don't reveal
Where you'd rather be...

(In school)?

Greta B. Lipson

GA1417

Activities

- The poem "My Enemy, My Friend" captures an experience that many people recognize. Have you ever had a serious falling-out with a close friend that you regretted deeply? Perhaps later, after tempers died down, there seemed to be no way of undoing the damage. Do you believe there is some way of changing this final course of events? What would your advice be to the person in the poem? Predict what could happen after a written apology?

- The poem "My Enemy, My Friend" is written as an English sonnet. It consists of fourteen lines, arranged as three quatrains and a couplet. The quatrains usually establish the idea or the problem, while the couplet usually serves as a summary statement, a final comment, or a philosophical stance. Here is a famous sonnet by William Shakespeare. It is marked off so that, if you are up to the challenge, you may want to try your hand at writing your own.

Shall I compare thee to a summer's day?	a
Thou art more lovely and more temperate:	b
Rough winds do shake the darling buds of May,	a
And summer's lease hath all too short a date:	b
Sometime too hot the eye of heaven shines,	c
And often is his gold complexion dimm'd;	d
And every fair from fair sometime declines,	c
By chance or nature's changing course untrimm'd	d
But thy eternal summer shall not fade	e
Nor lose possession of that fair thou ow'st;	f
Nor shall death brag thou wanderest in his shade,	e
When in eternal lines to time thou grow'st;	f
So long as men can breathe or eyes can see,	g
So long lives this and this gives life to thee.	g

GA1417

My Enemy, My Friend

I heard that you were back in our hometown.
Have you reflected through these passing years?
We were the very best of friends around,
Emotions roil to contemplate you near.

Do you feel pain from our old bitter fight?
I can't decide who did the grievous wrong,
Or who it was whose cause was in the right
Nor did it matter much, once you were gone.

Will you forget we gave each other grief?—
I wish to mend our breach in hopeful dreams
To still regret and give my soul relief
Be mine again, dear friend, in healing scenes.

When anger waned—I knew what I had lost
So unprepared was I to pay the cost.*

Greta B. Lipson

*Greta B. Lipson and Jane A. Romatowski, *Calliope: A Handbook of 47 Poetic Forms and Figures of Speech*, Good Apple, Inc., Carthage, Illinois, 1981, pp. 48-54.

41A

GA1417

Activities

• It is possible that as boring as a textbook may be for you, there are some students who learn best by reading. However, you should know that many years ago an educator came up with the idea of "cognitive mapping," meaning that each student's style of learning was analyzed so that it could be matched to a teacher's style which was similar. It was assumed that, having done this, the student could learn more successfully and the teacher could teach successfully. For the fun of it, draw a "cognitive map" showing the peculiarities of your brain and its fascinating pathways to learning. Display all of these brainy works of art. Award a prize to the most innovative mind map.

• You should know your own study habits better than anyone else does. If you had to identify the most effective way you learn, what would that be? Do you learn by listening, by reading a text, or by reviewing material out loud to a learning partner? There are oral learners and aural learners. Imagine you are a teacher writing up an analytical report of a student's learning habits (the student is you). For the record, be as accurate as you can be.

• Many people believe that if you want to learn something well, you should have to teach it! Your assignment will be to try to organize and execute a lesson. Decide on a topic you would like to teach. Keep the subject matter small and manageable. Make out a lesson plan as if you were a student teacher in training for the profession. Organize your plan as follows:

☐ Lesson: Making a peanut butter and jelly sandwich
☐ Objective: Learning to follow directions
☐ Motivation: How will you introduce the topic to capture interest?
☐ What materials must you have to teach the lesson?
☐ Procedure: Exactly how will you communicate the information
and what will the students do responsively–discuss, write, etc.?
☐ Bring the lesson to closure. How?
☐ Evaluate: Did the students learn? How will you measure their achievement? What was good? What was bad? How would you teach the lesson next time?

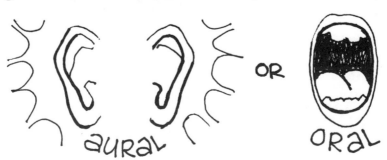

Open This Book and Die!

Dear Publisher:

Tell the committee that wrote this book
That I just took another look
At the pages and pages stuffed inside—

I collapsed in despair and really cried!

It's boring, dense and narcoleptic
It's mirthless, cold and antiseptic.

The text is not at all terrific
It gives one gas and is terribly cryptic
It zaps the brain cells of the class
In the annals of boredom—it's rotten for laughs.

It's leaden, sodden and uninspired
I warn again it'll make you tired
In the merciless depths of this swampish text
You will die a horrific, beastly death!

If you want a definition of *soporific*
Reading this text will be most specific!

Greta B. Lipson

Activities

• The point of the exercise using the poem "Deadly ABC's" is that it is possible to begin with a structured format that easily blossoms into a creative project. Using the pattern of this poem, construct your own wild poem. End with a paragraph which may help explain what is taking place and may also add to the madness of the concept. The trick is not to reject any ideas but simply let them flow. The poem will take over by itself!

• There are many other surprising activities that start with the alphabet. One of these, conceived by the poet Paul West, is called "Alphabet Poetry." According to his formula, the writer focuses on a particular topic such as fashion, then selects words to capture that topic, arranged in ABC order. The final step is the decision about how many words to place on a line. Shoot for colorful words! Here is an example.

Fashion
Aristocratic belts,
cute dresses, exquisite fabric gloves,
hats, Indian jewelry,
knits,
luscious mohair nightshirts

• Use every letter in the alphabet to develop a self-profile. Underline every consecutive letter which helps express your personality.
Example:

Me, Myself, and I

A   Lots of kids think I am a natural <u>athlete</u>
B   They call me a <u>baseball</u> freak
C   My voice can also be heard in <u>choir</u> practice
D   I am a <u>dog</u> lover

GA1417

Deadly ABC's

A always start with a theme
B before you begin to write an alphabet poem be–
C certain that the topic inspires you to create
D dozens of ideas
E enough to
F fill a page to overflowing–then
G go for it with
H humor, if you wish–or serious or dangerous
I intent!
J just give it your best shot
K knowing full well that you may not succeed at first–but that's
L life!
M many times you just go through the tedious, dull motions of creating,
N not knowing what dynamite will flow
O out of your sickly, sluggish
P pencil when
Q quietly, quickly, quixotically an uninvited torrent of quivering
R riotous, rollicking, rip roaring ideas explode like
S shooting stars threatening to explode your head when your
T teacher rushes to your side to stanch the tide of
U umpteen, unlimited ideas, larger than life–thoughts, impressions and
V visual images–which suddenly take the form of giant flowers, all of
W which are inundating the class in an inexplicable creeping growth. It is an
X xtraordinary brilliant display of giant flowering plants of
Y yellow, orange, red, white and blue luminous blossoms like
Z zinnias, azaleas, daisies, primroses, abronia villosa in monster proportions…

    The merciless flowers threaten to smother the room–and all its students. They are beginning to cry plaintively, as they disappear slowly under the undulating surface of giant petals, stems, and horticultural dementia. They beg for your explanation! "Why? Why have you created these fiendish flowers to destroy us?"

    To which you respond: "C D B?"*

Greta B. Lipson

---

*William Steig, *C D B!* Simon & Schuster, New York, 1968.

GA1417

Activities

- A one-minute kiss burns up twenty-six calories, a Hershey's Kiss® adds twenty-five calories. Write a short, short story based upon that information.

- Look up the definition of *love* in the dictionary. Does it help clarify the meaning of love, from your point of view? Discuss other abstract words.

- What does the word *love* mean in each of the following contexts? How are they different? With a study partner, write out the differences.
  - ☐ A parent
  - ☐ Grandparents
  - ☐ A boyfriend
  - ☐ Love of money
  - ☐ Love of power
  - ☐ Love of country
  - ☐ A girlfriend
  - ☐ A child
  - ☐ Love of your bike, motorcycle, or car
  - ☐ Love of freedom

- Research Eros and Cupid and be able to tell some Greek or Roman myths regarding their role in the act of falling in love. For the sheer pain and frustration of lovers, find and read the Greek myth of Pyramus and Thisbe about the two Assyrian lovers who lived next door to each other from birth. Who are some other famous lovers?

- What is the etymology (the source and development) of the word *love*? Does the origin of the word help explain the concept for you? List or discuss some of the more interesting details of the origins of the word *love*.

- How did the heart become the symbol which represents love? How about the stomach or liver or brain or nose? How would advertisements for Sweetest Day or other lovers' holidays be represented without the heart? Produce such a romantic advertisement.

- If you want very much to be seen with a person of the opposite sex because you are dying to impress your friends, does that mean you are in love with that person or is there some other self-serving influence at work? Explain.

44

"I Love You" in 26 Languages

Te quiero.	(Spanish)	French	amour
Ich liebe dich.	(German)	Spanish	amor
Je t'aime.	(French)	Italian	amore
Ja cie kocham.	(Polish)	Portuguese	amor
Ti amo.	(Italian)	Rumanian	iubire
As tave myliu.	(Lithuanian)	German	Liebe
Cakam te.	(Macedonian)	Dutch	liefde
Volim te.	(Serbian)	Swedish	karlek
Une dua ty.	(Albanian)	Danish	elskov
	(Sign Language)	Norwegian	kjaerlighet
		Polish	milosc
		Czech	laska
		Serbo-Croat.	ljubav
		Hungarian	szeretet
		Finnish	rakkaus
		Turkish	ask, sevgi
		Indonesian	tjinta
		Esperanto	amo
		Russian	lyubof
		Greek	asa'pi
		Arabic	houb
		Hebrew	ahavah
		Yiddish	libe
		Japanese	ai
		Swahili	upendo

44A

GA1417

Activities

- The poem "Smoke, Cough, Spit, Puff" is a pantoum which is a fifteenth century Malayan poetic form. For complete directions on how to write this style of poem, see activities page 27. Write a "smoking" pantoum expressing your own attitude about the habit.

- What are the dangers of smoking? Research the information and develop a class "Fact Sheet." Document every fact you have collected by giving the source, date, page, etc. Post it in the room until you are absolutely certain that your Fact Sheet is all-inclusive. Why is the date of any information important?

- States like Kentucky, which raise tobacco, lag behind other states in establishing no-smoking bans in public places, because tobacco is critical to their economic security. How would you feel about this if you lived in a community where people (including you) earned their living by working in the tobacco industry? Think this over very carefully before expressing an opinion. It is easy to make decisions which affect other people profoundly but do not affect our own personal security directly.

- The numbers of people who smoke is moving downward. In 1991 only 25 percent of Americans were smoking, with the nonsmoking trend showing more progress than experts thought would happen. The National Cancer Institute expects that by the year 2000 only 17 percent of the population will be smoking. What is the figure this year? Where did you find these statistics?

- When smoking is not permitted in the workplace, some smokers feel that their rights as American citizens are not being respected. Other workers–who do not smoke–claim that research shows that breathing other people's smoke causes disease just as if one were actually smoking. Imagine that you are the boss of a factory and you hold a meeting to settle the issue between the two factions. Each declare their rights as American citizens. Each side has a chance to express its views. Role-play this heated meeting. How will it be resolved? Are people's rights being violated? Whose?

45

Smoke, Cough, Spit, Puff

1	Hey! cool customer puffing smoke in the air
2	Dragging on the fatal weed
3	Wanta lay odds the fates will get you?
4	Your lungs are a sponge filled with noxious tar
5-2	Dragging on the fatal weed
6	Life is short and wears away
7-4	Your lungs are a sponge filled with noxious tar
8	Ugly word–cough, vile word–phlegm
9-6	Life is short and wears away
10	Gasp for air later through a skinny reed.
11-8	Ugly word–cough, vile word–phlegm
12	Go for it–you're adult. Die like one too.
13-10	Gasp for air later through a skinny reed.
14	What did the Surgeon General say?
15-12	Go for it–you're adult. Die like one too.
16 -1	Hey, cool customer puffing smoke in the air!*

Greta B. Lipson

*The first line of the poem must be used as the last line of the poem, wherever you choose to end it.

GA1417

Activities

• The sexist notion that only females are competent in the kitchen and only men enjoy the status of chefs in professional settings is long outdated! Cooking is a practical life skill! Everyone should be able to shop for food, and prepare it adequately well without mother around to tie on your bib and tucker. (What on Earth is a tucker?) Have you or someone else in your family ever had an outrageous experience in the kitchen out of sheer stupidity? Give the class a treat and recount the episode in detail.

• Many people have a "comfort food" which they eat when they are in need of emotional support. For some it may be hot chocolate with a marshmallow bobbing around. For others it may be chicken noodle soup. Describe your "comfort food" on one page with a heartfelt title. What is it? What does it do for you? What circumstances lead up to your need for this food (other than hunger)?

• When you are camping out, the meals prepared in a heavy cast-iron pot over an open fire can be a wonderfully hearty experience. Do some research on your own and discover a "stew pot survival concoction" which can be prepared in your own kitchen as well. Can you find some recipe books written just for campers? If you find a mind-boggling recipe from venturesome people in the wild, write it out on an index card and contribute it to a collection of similar gastronomic delights. Boiled muskrat, anyone?

• For an aromatic, down home, rib sticking, soul-satisfying soup, write to G. Lipson, P.O. Box 3452, Ann Arbor, Michigan 48106. Just ask for Chuckie's Chunky Chicken Barley Soup. Enclose a self-addressed, stamped business envelope.

Zuppa Soup

The topic for today is nourishing soup
But we don't mean commercial goop
But really-oh, truly-oh, homemade soup;

Soup offers gastronomic thrills
And an opportunity for survival skills
Everyone needs to learn to cook
Especially without a cooking book

Use nice chicken to make the soup
Add veggies and dill in a spicy group
Toss in barley—keep stirring the pot
The recipe's foolproof, so make a lot

Soup is "Poor Folk's Penicillin"
Good for adults and little chillen
A good pot of the stuff tastes like ambrosia
It travels your system from your head to your toes-a

Men, women and children can learn to make
A wonderful soup that takes the cake
So when your crazed family troops into the house
Declaring their hunger in thunderous shouts
Rescue that starving gluttonous group
And offer them some of your marvelous soup!

Greta B. Lipson

GA1417

Activities

- "Home Cento" uses a poetic form which is also called patchwork poetry. Cento can be a challenging activity to put together, particularly for those who enjoy playing with language. The poem may be constructed in two ways. Select each line from a different, already existing, poem. The challenge comes in finding lines which work well together and which make sense when read as a total poem. The poem may be nonrhyming or rhyming; for rhyming poems the rhyme scheme is aa, bb, cc.

I saw a ship a-sailing,	a	(Mother Goose)
Blue sky prevailing.	a	(William Wordsworth)
Sweet day, so cool, so calm, so bright.	b	(George Herbert)
Welcome all wonders in one sight.	b	(Richard Crashaw)
On this green bank, by thee, soft stream	c	(Ralph Waldo Emerson)
Was it a vision—or a waking dream?	c	(John Keats)

Assembled by Jane Romatowski*

Patience and love of the search are necessary for this task. The search makes a good cooperative experience for small group collaboration.

- The plight of homeless people in America is a severe and growing problem. It is hard to imagine that conditions, which may be beyond one's control, can force people out into the streets. Homeless children and adults live in cardboard boxes, abandoned buildings, under bridges, and other hidden places. If, on a cold winter night, a homeless person came to your door, what would you do? Think hard and honestly about this. Discuss everyone's answer.

- In your own words explain one or more of these quotes.
  - ☐ "Be it ever so humble, there's no place like home."
  - ☐ "Home is where the heart is."
  - ☐ "It takes a heap o' livin' in a house t' make it home."
  - ☐ "Home is my safe haven from the cruel world."
  - ☐ "Home, 99 $^{44}/_{100}$% Sweet Home." (Ogden Nash)

Now make up your own quotable quote about home.

---

*See *Calliope: A Handbook of Poetic Forms and Figures of Speech* by G. Lipson and J. Romatowski, Good Apple, Inc., Carthage, IL © 1981, p. 87.

Home Cento*

Home, home from the horizon far and clear	(Alice Meyernell)
How beautiful it was that one bright day	(Hawthorne)
Family story tells, and it was told true	(Anne Sexton)
Memory of time is here imprisoned	(Stanley J. Kunitz)
Home's not merely four square walls	(Charles Swain)
Comfort when work seems difficult	(Isaiah–Bible)
Since fret and care are everywhere	(unknown)
In an old house there is always listening	(T.S. Eliot)
Home of my heart, I sing of thee!	(H.S. Lyster)
If you're sad at heart, take a trip there tonight.	(Andrew B. Sterling)

*See *The Columbia Granger's Index to Poetry*, 9th edition, 1990, The Columbia University Press, New York. (For titles, first lines, and authors)

47A

Activities

• Organize a panel discussion relative to the issues that are suggested in the poem. You may assume the role of a good friend, parent, teacher, principal, professor, college coach, high school coach, agent, employer or whomever you choose. Address one or more problems in high school and college athletic programs. Select a moderator for the discussion. Add any other topics chosen for discussion to the following list.

- ☐ No Pass, No Play
- ☐ Why Athletes Can't Read
- ☐ From High School Fame to Personal Failure
- ☐ University Presidents Must Have More Control
- ☐ Intercollegiate Athletics
- ☐ Only One out of Every One Hundred College Athletes Gets into Professional Sports
- ☐ Athletes Must Get an Education and Must Graduate
- ☐ Consistently Allowing Athletes into Easy Courses Is Against Academic Ethics
- ☐ Athletes Who Are Obviously Unable to Succeed Academically in College Should Not Be Courted by College Athletic Departments
- ☐ Alumni Like Successful Athletic Programs
- ☐ TV's Impact on Sports Has Been Enormous and Is Big Business

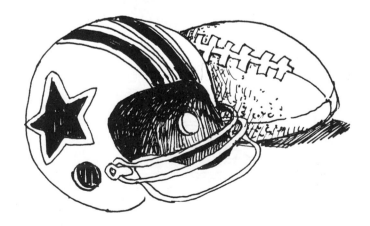

GA1417

Heracles, Hercules, Harry Keyes

Listen up Heracles, Hercules, Harry Keyes!

You were young, you were strong
You could do no wrong
You were favored by the gods
And we knew it.

School uniform with blazing borders
Young athlete of the highest order
Elegant body, handsome face
Breathtaking skills
And incredible grace
And we loved you.

You inspired the students at the game
With glorious power on a field of fame
Your brilliant victory won the day
Our lusty response was a roaring display
And you loved it.

Yet—there comes a loss of celebrity
As always, the athlete's moment wanes
Another inevitable wrenching change
What do the fans give in exchange?
We forget you.

What will it be for you, Harry Keyes?
Beyond the transitory phase
Beyond the shouting of the crowds,
Beyond the heady extravagant praise,
Beyond the love, beyond the glory
Will yours be another typical story?

We owe you something, Harry Keyes.
For excellence and stunning plays
We owe you something beyond adulation
We owe you a decent education.

Greta B. Lipson

48A

GA1417

Activities

- On the following page, why does the content of Dimitar's statement surprise us? What does our surprise have to do with our expectations of women as teachers or leaders? Explain why you think the premise of Dimitar's statement is true or false? Who was Golda Meir? (She was a schoolteacher in Milwaukee, Wisconsin, who later became Prime Minister of Israel from 1969-1974.) Who was Margaret Thatcher? Indira Gandhi? How does the word *stereotype* relate to the subject of equal opportunity?

- Write a paragraph or a phrase about a person in such a way that the gender of the character comes as a surprise. For example, the plane landed in the treacherous weather to the whooping and hollering of the grateful passengers. They thanked the pilot noisily as they disembarked, and she flashed a smile back that said, "You're welcome." What role or occupation or profession did the central character of your piece have? Do women fill those roles currently? If they do, why do we still have trouble seeing them as carpenters, flyers, war correspondents, symphony orchestra conductors, or accomplished athletes?

- On the chalkboard make one list of personality traits which you consider to be strictly masculine. Make another list of traits which you consider to be strictly feminine. Discuss those traits. Are there crossovers? Do these characteristics truly belong to one sex only?

- Select an interesting human interest item from a newspaper, a news magazine, or a piece of literature. Copy the descriptive paragraph or two, but change the sex of the main character in your selection. Does something radical happen? What happens and why?

- What personality characteristics are leadership qualities? Write a paragraph to support the statement that the sex of a person does not determine leadership abilities. Research the names of women leaders in modern times.

- March is Women's History Month. For information and materials, contact the National Women's History Project, 7738 Bell Rd., Windsor, CA 95492, Phone: 707-838-6000. Learn about great women in history.

Equal Opportunity

I think woman should be concidered for presidentcy. Because this is free country. Everybody can be president of United States but just this people Who are citizens of U.S. of America. Woman can do all what man can do. **Ms. Barclaw** will be president of the United Stats of America because she is **smart** woman. Every people who are smarts can be president of the U.S. of America.

by Dimitar Tzonkov
April, 1991

This lyrical expression, in praise of women's capabilities, and the opportunities in a free country, was written in 1991, by fourteen-year-old Dimitar Tzonkov, a Bulgarian immigrant, who had been in this country for barely three months. He wrote this heartfelt piece while attending Chatterton Middle School in the Fitzgerald School System in Warren, Michigan. He was a student in the bilingual program and greatly admired his teacher, Ms. Geraldine Barclay, who was the coordinator of the program.

Poems That Speak for Themselves

GA1417

Rites of Passage

Childhood is a long, tough haul
At a critical age when you're grown and all
You take a ferry on a strange short ride
Where you grow up fast on the other side.

The ride is called the "Rites of Passage"
But you don't need a bit of baggage
The sign says, "Adult Entitlements Here!"
And you'll rush right over with expectant cheer.

You can hardly wait to buy your ticket
From the man behind the sticky wicket
There's a very high bridge that you gotta cross over
And once you do it seems you're in clover.

After a long, rough, ferryboat ride
You want some treats on the other side
You ask for a hot dog and golden fries
But they laugh till they nearly split their sides.

"You don't get nothin' for free over here
And the cost of things is mighty dear.
Nobody's here to help you pay
'Cause when you're grown up it's always this way.
So set your clock for the break of day—
Our motto here is work and no play
You'll be working nonstop for 65 years
Now straighten out—and dry those tears!"

You ask, "Where's the good times and the grown-up fun–?
The rollicking, frolicking games in the sun?"
They said, "You must be thinking of a different place.
This here's for adults and the old rat race!"

Well you sure weren't ready for such responsibility
So you rush back to the ticket man with real humility:
"I wanna go back to the other side. I made a mistake when I took this ride!"
But he shook his head and gave me his answer,
"Too late kid! We punched your transfer!"

Greta B. Lipson

GA1417

Teacher, Teacher

Teacher, teacher
Why do you teach,
When the world belies everything you preach?

All mothers do not love their children
Nor do all men love their brothers
Nor are all our children protected as the hope for the future
Nor do we guard the public trust
Nor do we practice equality
Or guarantee a decent life for all
Regardless of race, color, creed or gender.
Nor do we live in harmony, free of war
Nor do we cherish and protect nature's bountiful gifts

Do you teach for what is real?
Do you teach for the "ideal"?
Will it frighten or prepare me?

Teacher, teacher
Why do you teach,
When the world betrays everything you teach?
Where is the nobility of which you speak?

What source replenishes your spirit?

Greta B. Lipson

52

GA1417

Use It and Abuse It!

PSST!
Over here kid.
How would you like to get a fast high, a humdinger charge, a good buzz
A rush you never in this world knew existed?
Here's something to sniff, snort, smoke, drink or shoot
It'll put you out of your gourd, out of your skin, out of control!

Then later you can slobber, puke, or...
Get that heart pumping till it breaks through your chest
Or would you rather have a stroke and spasm yourself into lifetime paralysis?

We can arrange a cockeyed alcoholic joy ride for you and your best friends
And then you can smash them to hell, forever, in one great chicken livered
Challenge on the freeway! Wow!
Now you're talkin' big-time fun!

Hey!
Don't let "the stuff" scare you man.
Remember you can always take it or leave it.
You're the boss of *You*–no matter what anybody says.
And don't forget it.

What's that crap?–pay a price?
That's slop for wimps and snotty nose do-gooders.
You can forget school
Forget the future
Forget the family
Forget keeping your brains and eyeballs and guts and legs and arms in place
Forget everything and everybody
Give it a chance and pretty soon nothing else will matter anyway!

Take a chance
Be cool
Meet you at the body dumpster,
Sooner or later.

That's my hangout.

Greta B. Lipson

What–Me Worry?

Many kids, contrary to adult expectations,
Have a lot of worries
But not me!

Other kids are riddled with fear
Like holes in a block of Swiss cheese.
But not me!

Why should I worry about
Being humiliated,
Looking ugly,
Sounding dumb,
Moving,
Not being asked to the dance,
Going blind,
Having an accident in class,
Seeing my parents argue,
Fitting in,
Being on the outside, looking in,
Dressing wrong,
Getting good grades,
Earning money,
Not knowing what I will be when I grow up,
Being cool,
Not having a single good friend,
Parent/teacher approval,
The facts of life
        and death.

How do I know other kids are riddled with fear?
I read a lot and besides–they told me

But me, personally–
I don't have a worry in the world.

Greta B. Lipson

GA1417

Little Bro

It's way past time that I told little bro
That he truly impresses me.
He's a master resolver, a smart problem solver
Yet, an ordinary guy, so it seems.

Brought up together—two birds of a feather
From a nest in the same family tree.
But I knew from the start, in my heart of deep hearts,
That no one was smarter than he.

With whom would you want to be lost in the woods?
Who's most likely to help you get out?
Out of self-preservation—without hesitation,
"Little Bro"—in one voice—we all shout.

From where comes the depth and the breadth of his brains
So profoundly revealed and resplendent?
From where comes his "stuff" without any strain,
So cerebral and so independent?

Hey nipper, hey kid, hey little bro blue,
Whenever did this come to be?
You are doctor B. now—with a wirey brown beard,
With a 'scope and an M.D. degree!

Under your much beloved baseball cap
Resides both the boy and the man
Fulfilling a promise we have come to expect
A proud role in the great cosmic plan.

Greta B. Lipson

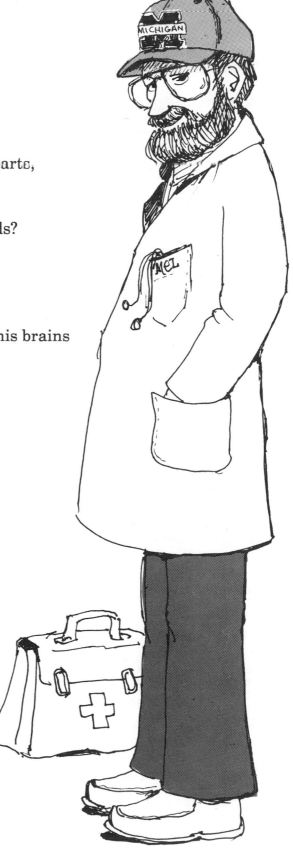

Her Royal Highness

My sister's story is that she is really a princess!
But when she was little she was stolen by
      short, little Gypsies.

Like them–she wore a kerchief on her head with
Flashing spangles–pulled tightly over her straight blonde hair.
They loved her a lot and told her she was divinely beautiful.
So, of course she stayed with them.

They were chubby and short and out of her sincere feeling for them
She stayed short too.
They loved to eat and she learned their lustful ways with food
And loads of it.
These fat little Gypsies were thrilled to be alive (they didn't know they were poor).
They laughed until their abode rocked with their resounding belly laughs.
So my sister learned to be funny because they admired people of mirth.

She forsook her regal raiment and dressed as a Gypsy should:
In twirling colorful skirts and silks and satins with jangling bracelets
And ornate earrings that stretched her ear lobes down.

And though she never forgets her royal birthright as a princess
She stays with these short little Gypsies
Never returning to her natural parents, the King and Queen.

My sister looks like a Gypsy–that part is true.
But I don't believe the rest of it.
Do you?

      Greta B. Lipson

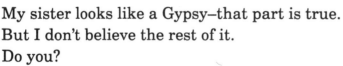

Space Cadet

You must remember this
She only seems like an alien
From another planet.
She smiles kindly at everyone–(even at scuzz balls).
She is enthralled by math
And madly in love with science.

$$2x + y = z$$

The butt of jokes (because she's different).
Eager to help everyone (when she lands, that is)!
Indifferent to the tyranny of fashion,
     Fads
     Popularity
     What's in
     Who's out
Or all the other junk we care about.

$$3.14159265359$$

She sees the world as if
She were floating free outside the planet
With a tether fastened 'round her waist
To pull her back to Earth.

But aren't we lucky
There are more than a few of her around–
To write novels and paint pictures
And compose music and choreograph dance
And do science and mathematics.

She actually understands particle physics (and is only in high school!)
Let's count our blessings–and value our free spirits
And all of those fey souls around
Who are not herd-bound!

Greta B. Lipson

The Scientific Future Times announced on Monday, Jan. 7, 2025, the appointment of Dr. Rachel Rose, as Director of the International Institute of Theoretical Physics at Fairfield State University. She specializes in relativity, supergravity, optical parallel computing, solar energy and astrophysics.

GA1417

Ture or Flase Test

SPELLING BUGABOOS

I **red sumwear** that lots of **peepul**
Don't **no** how to **spel**.
It's **knot** because we aren't smart
But **sum** words just don't **jel**.

"Look it up you **sillie** fool"
Is what I **hait** to **here**
Without the proper **speling**
The task **wood** take a **yeer**.

If you **tide** up all **goud spellerz**
And **lasht** them **two** a **trea**,
All those **despert** boys and **grils**
Wood be calling out **four** me

Knot because I **spel goud**
Knot because I'm **brite**
Butt my warm and **kindlee attitood**
Makes everything **seam write**.

I'm **wurking** on my **speling**
I'll get **bettor** in a **wile**
Butt if **eye** try and **fale**
Reward my **effert** with a smile.

Greta B. Lipson

Grade Pressure

An "A" is ginger peachy,
So straight and strong and tall
Its muscle sets off lightning sparks
It's glamor lights the halls.

Now–"B" looks nice and fullsome
An adequate good show
It shows the world your brain's in place.
With promises to grow.

"C" is getting flatter
Like a tire losing air
The signs of struggle showing
It tells us you're just fair!

Now "D" looks like it's limping
With signs of real disgrace
There's still a chance to rally,
Though–
There's failure in its face.

Oh "E"–Yes "E" is dying
It's death knell's loud and clear
And now, I fear, it's clearly time
To get your act in gear!

The fight for grades continues
No nothing gives you ease
The battle is incessant
No one promised you a breeze.

Greta B. Lipson

GA1417

Advice Column

My advice is written for you poor souls
With dreadful problems you often pose
Read my column every day
And learn from it in every way

Your problems arrive in a multitude
Some relative to pulchritude

No problem's too big
No problem's too small
We'll read all your letters
And answer them all.

We've heard from you often
Right down through the years
You're pained and imperfect
One can tell by your fears

Let me tell all you cynics
Who think we pretend
To care for dear hearts
And help them to mend

We'll ration compassion
Give out with advice
Just follow our column
We'll respond in a thrice

My booklet explains what is tried and true
Our aim is to remedy what makes you blue.
Check off your affliction, your concerns and your woes
You'll get back my answer
When your buck you enclose.

Your humble servant, Dr. Jeepers.

Greta B. Lipson

GA1417

About Family

Tell about family
where love is born
     Comfort inside
     Secure and warm

Wonder of wonders
that I belong
     In this vast world
     In a place that is strong

Celebrate ties
that bind my days
     To loving people
     In countless ways

Give thanks to a family
with nurturing grace
     That holds me close
     In sweet embrace

Tell about family
where love is born
     Comfort inside
     Secure and warm.

          Greta B. Lipson

Grandparental Connection
A Villanelle*

1	My gram and grandfather offer love like no other
2	Their small house for me is a port in the storm
3	It took me a while to enjoy and discover.
4	They envelop my spirit with nurturing cover
5	A snug and safe harbor in a place that is warm
6-1	My gram and grandfather offer love like no other
7	Their welcome is kind. I am never a bother
8	I can hide in their house, castaway from a storm
9-3	It took me a while to enjoy and discover–
10	They reach out the same to my father and mother.
11	There's a range of the parts and the roles they perform
12-1	My gram and grandfather offer love like no other
13	My spirit once failed and they helped me recover
14	Like a failing young bird my strength was reborn
15-3	It took me a while to enjoy and discover–
16	Their devoted support is the gift I uncovered
17	It is there for the family and it waits unadorned
18-1	My gram and grandfather offer love like no other
19-3	It took me a while to enjoy and discover.

Greta B. Lipson

---

*The form of this poem is a villanelle, invented by the French poet, Jean Passerat in the late 1500's. There are usually six stanzas. The first five stanzas are three lines long. The sixth stanza has four lines. The rhyme scheme is a, b, a throughout the entire poem. In the last stanza there is a variation which is a, b, a, a. There are only two rhymes allowed throughout the poem. It is a brain buster. Lines 1 and 3 are repeated according to the pattern above.

GA1417

Don't Holler

I may do dumb things but I'm honest and true
So this is a favor I'm asking of you–
Whatever you do–**Don't Holler!**

My guilt is enough, so don't make it tough
Reproach me and ground me–instruct me and hound me,
But whatever you do–**Don't Holler!**

Keep me inside. Deprive me of air
Threaten and scare me
Mess up my hair
However you punish, I'll consider it fair
But whatever you do–**Don't Holler!**

I'll polish the car and wax all the doors
Shine up the windows and scrub all the floors
I'll attend to the garbage–take it out every week
You won't hear from me–no, nary a peep
I'll sit with the kids, the dog and the cat
I'll never act big or sound like a rat
But whatever you do–**Don't Holler!**

Tell me to stop being mean and sarcastic
I'll get pious and sweet–It'll just be fantastic
No one denies that I did a dumb thing, I'll reform and repent
It won't cost you a cent

Do all of the things, psychologically sound
And sooner or later I'll come around
There are good ways and bad ways to castigate
But there is one way that I earnestly hate.
So–whatever you do–**Don't Holler!**

Remember the punishment should fit the crime
And that's the best way to finish this rhyme.

Greta B. Lipson

GA1417

Fink of the Road

He's a zero, a nothing
But oh how he drives!
The big dude of the road
A hometown surprise

The most daring of drivers
Baby boy at the wheel
To listen to him
One would think he's some deal!

Safety's for chickens
He knows that for sure
He drives like a lunatic
For him that's the lure!

Clear byways and highways
Get rid of the rest
The roads are for him
He thinks he's the best

Scare them and dare them
Is his big surprise
But one day for sure
He'll meet his demise

He makes drivers sore
Like a boil on the neck
With more time and dumbness
He'll end up in a wreck

We wait for that final smart alecky flip
The one that will win him his final car trip
We pray when that time comes he'll be on his own
And everyone else had the luck to be home.

Greta B. Lipson

64

GA1417

Praise Pays

We bring to your attention
That we all need special mention
Though we can't be topnotch winners every day

I'll give it to you straight
Try to make kids feel great
In those most important moments day by day

'Cause kind words said in phrases
And these phrases full of praises
Will enhance our self-esteem in every way!

Paste a star upon the forehead
Of a kid who's usually horrid
Then stand back and watch the fireworks display!

Greta B. Lipson

GA1417

Gotta Dance

Fox trot
Lambada
Waltz, tango and hop
Fricasee, chicken, jitterbug, and sock
Samba, mambo, break dance and jerk
Lindy, twist, monkey, tap dance and quirk

Light up your fuse
Loose as a goose
Swing it and sway it
Don your tarboosh
Supple your muscles
Make those joints loose
Trip the fantastic
And shake your caboose!

Greta B. Lipson

GA1417

Tell Us a Story

Once upon a time:

Tell tales short and tall
To frighten or delight
I yearn to hear them all

Romance is my first choice
Tell it warm and end it right
A fairy tale dream
A whimsical delight

Next give me scary stuff
Adventures full of gore
Send shivers up my spine
Blood oozing on the floor.

Pull tears from out my eyes
With tales of wretched fate
With people full of spite
And creatures full of hate

Let's get to outer space
In a future so sublime
With androids human-like
And technoids so divine

Now tickle funny bones
With lots of belly laughs
Tell yarns of clowns and fools
Who work an ancient craft

Speak of generals and queens
On battlefields of war
Who play strategic games
And keep their deadly score.

Once upon a time
In stories you design!

Greta B. Lipson

67

GA1417

Other People's Troubles

They gathered in the village square—hopeful, expectant
The townsfolk were sombre and composed. Some outsiders had come.
For it was "Burden Day."
On this day it was possible to trade other people's problems for your own
Even the cats and dogs were there—quietly resigned to human foibles.
A stout clothesline was pulled tightly from one end of the brick lined street,
Past the center fountain—to the extreme and far reaches of the town.

Thrown over the line were white muslin sheets, snapping in the wind.
People of all ages took their respective positions in front of the sheets.
Others, (more sophisticated) stood apart and watched silently.
Each person began to write in heavy dark strokes, a list of personal burdens,
Problems, bad luck, hardship, private grief and sorrow, lost love, poor health.
Some participants, more reflective, took longer than the others.
No matter—it was a day for collective patience and the revelation of
          profound troubles.
Everyone understood. There was no jostling.

Having completed their lists on the flapping muslin sheets there was a brief
          intermission before the serious business began.
The silent reading commenced at a signal. Individuals drifted from one
          marked sheet—to the next and the next and the next
They read the linear burdens of others—in melancholy detail.
There were sighs, unashamed tears, exclamations and occasional laughter.

The blessed lure of this day was that if you chose to trade someone else's
Grief for your own—your wish would be granted—by some magic force
And your life could be better and less painful. But there were no guarantees.
Dusk came.
The reading continued. Some went back to read again, a list that held, (perhaps)
          a meager promise.

The crowd thinned—drifting home in different directions
In the darkness the local mummers came in their costumes
They took down the sheets to use as stories for future dramas.
No one had chosen another's grief.
This was no surprise.
The older ones knew.
It was the same every year.

Greta B. Lipson

GA1417

Reverend Spoonerisms*

Oh, Reverend Spooner, you're such a delight
Though your words, transposed, are a bit of a fright!

"May I sew you to another sheet?"
(May I show you to another seat?)

"Sir, you have tasted a whole worm. "
(Sir, you have wasted a whole term.)

"You have hissed my mystery lessons."
(You have missed my history lessons.)

"All hail to the kinkering congs!"
(All hail to the conquering kings!)

"Now that is a well boiled icicle."
(Now that is a well oiled bicycle.)

"Let us drink to the queer old Dean."
(Let us drink to the dear old queen.)

"There is a roaring pain."
(There is a pouring rain.)

Your distortions seem a clever game
You are known for all your blunders
Your wacky words brought you instant fame
Is it really any wonder?

Greta B. Lipson

* Reverend William Archibald Spooner (1844-1930) was an English clergyman who taught at New College, Oxford, England.
He is said to have delighted his students with his amusing, but unintentional style of transposing sounds.

GA1417

Snacking at the Grisly Horror Show

We sat there, calm and cautious
While I felt myself get nauseous
With the cloying, clammy, claws–
Stretched on the screen

For this monster is so horrid
It's so gruesome, I abhor it
    Still I need a chocolate yummy
    If you please!

"IT" was rotting, retching, roaring
Not a single moment boring
    I would love a gooey gumdrop
    If you please!

Seeping pustules, wet and squishy
Sticky slime alive with fishies
    Would you pass the peanut clusters
    If you please!

"IT" was oozing sticky mallow
Like a mass of pukey tallow
    Would you share the buttered popcorn
    If you please!

Greta B. Lipson

GA1417

Beginnings and Endings

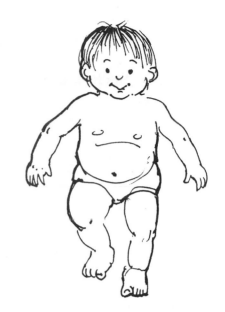

To begin with—
Everything has a beginning and everything has an ending.
My favorites, of course, are the beginnings
(Can someone please say something good about endings?)

Beginnings such as
The top of the first inning when the umpire says "Play ball!"
Crowding into the football stadium for the home game
Face off at the hockey game
Center jump with the basketball giants

I'll take appetizers for beginnings
Or a plateful of meat and potatoes if you don't start fancy
The first stirrings of a love affair
A baby's borning cry
New puppies in a box
Winning something—anything!
A second chance

The curtain going up in the theatre and the surge of the pit orchestra.
The lights going down at the movies with that compelling opening shot
Diving into a cool lake under a blazing summer sun
A first suit. A first party dress.
The family's new car (which could even be used)
Your new car (which is certainly used)
The first hopeful trip away from home and parents
A for-real paycheck earned by you and you alone!

Ahh, but what about endings?
Some good—some bad.

The last page of a fantastic book
The end of final exams (yeh)!
The last days of vacation
Goodbye to a summer romance
Dessert is a great ending!
And best of all—
Don't dare forget
GRADUATION DAY!

Greta B. Lipson

Suggested Readings

De Sisto, Michael. *Decoding Your Teenager*. New York: Wm. Morrow, 1991.

Deutsch, Babette. *Poetry Handbook: A Dictionary of Terms*. Fourth edition New York: Harper & Row, 1981.

Hopkins, Roy J. *Adolescence: The Transitional Years*. New York: Academic Press, a subsidiary of Harcourt Brace Jovanovich, 1983.

Lapides, Frederick R., and John T. Shawcross, editors. *Poetry and Its Conventions: An Anthology Examining Poetic Forms and Themes*. New York: Free Press, 1972.

Lehman, David, editor. *Ecstatic Occasions, Expedient Forms*. New York: Macmillan, 1987.

Lipson, Greta B. *A Book for All Seasons: 70 Poems, Lessons, Activities for Special Days*. Carthage, IL.: Good Apple, Inc., 1990.

Lipson, Greta B., and Jane Romatowski. *Calliope: A Handbook of 47 Poetic Forms and Figures of Speech*. Carthage, IL.: Good Apple, Inc., 1981.

Packard, William. *The Poets Dictionary: A Handbook of Prosody and Poetic Devices*. New York: Harper & Row, 1989.

Padgett, Ron, editor. *The Teachers and Writers Handbook of Poetic Forms*. New York: Teachers and Writers Collaborative, 1987.

Perrine, Lawrence. *Sound & Sense: An Introduction to Poetry*. Seventh edition New York: Harcourt, Brace, Jovanovich, 1987.

Sebranek, Patrick, et. al. *The Write Source*. Burlington, WI, The Write Source Publishers, 1987.

Untermeyer, Louis. *The Pursuit of Poetry*. New York: Simon & Schuster, 1969.

GA1417